EVALUATING THE
YEAR 2000 PROJECT

D1566001

EVALUATING THE YEAR 2000 PROJECT

A MANAGEMENT GUIDE FOR DETERMINING REASONABLE CARE

TIMOTHY BRAITHWAITE

JOHN WILEY & SONS, INC.

New York • Chichester • Weinheim • Brisbane • Singapore • Toronto

This book is printed on acid-free paper. ∞

Copyright© 1998 by John Wiley & Sons, Inc. All rights reserved.

Published simultaneously in Canada.

No part of this publication may be reproduced, stored in a
retrieval system or transmitted in any form or by any means,
electronic, mechanical, photocopying, recording, scanning or
otherwise, except as permitted under Sections 107 or 108 of the
1976 United States Copyright Act, without either the prior written
permission of the Publisher, or authorization through payment of
the appropriate per-copy fee to the Copyright Clearance Center,
222 Rosewood Drive, Danvers, MA 01923, (508) 750-8400,
fax (508) 750-4744. Requests to the Publisher for permission
should be addressed to the Permissions Department,
John Wiley & Sons, Inc., 605 Third Avenue, New York, NY
10158-0012, (212) 850-6011, fax (212) 850-6008,
E-Mail: PERMREQ@WILEY.COM.

This publication is designed to provide accurate and
authoritative information in regard to the subject
matter covered. It is sold with the understanding that
the publisher is not engaged in rendering
professional services. If professional advice or other
expert assistance is required, the services of a competent
professional person should be sought.

Library of Congress Cataloging in Publication Data:
Braithwaite, Timothy, 1942–
     Evaluating the year 2000 project : a management guide for determining reasonable care
/ Timothy Braithwaite.
        p.   cm.
     Includes bibliographical references and index.
     ISBN 0-471-25329-4 (pbk. : alk. paper)
     1. Year 2000 date conversion (Computer systems)   2. Software
maintenance—Management.   I. Title.
QA76.76.S64B73   1998
658.4'08—dc21   97-39021

Printed in the United States of America

10 9 8 7 6 5 4 3 2 1

ABOUT THE AUTHOR

Timothy B. Braithwaite has more than 30 years of experience in all aspects of automated data processing, communications, and information systems management. Currently director of Year 2000 Services for J. G. Van Dyke & Associates, he has managed data centers, software development projects, system planning and budgeting organizations, and has extensive experience in computer acquisition activities. His pioneering work in computer systems security and privacy resulted in his appointment to the Privacy Protection Study Commission in 1976 and his recruitment to be the first systems security officer for the Social Security Administration in 1978. He has a masters degree in technology management from American University and a bachelor of science degree in business administration from Rockhurst College.

CONTENTS

ACKNOWLEDGMENTS

I would like to thank Kelley Braithwaite, J. D., Thomas Crouch, Robert Driscoll, William Franklin, Steve Gordon, Belden Menkus, John O'Connor, and Marc Pearl, M. D. for contributions to this effort.

These individuals and many others identified issues unique to their professions—issues that must be taken into account when attempting to deal with the year 2000 computer crisis in a responsible and reasonable manner.

PREFACE

This book provides a high-level management review guide that can be used by company officers, boards of directors, government officials, line managers, and anyone else who has an interest in whether or not an organization can demonstrate reasonable care (RC) in its handling of the millennium "bug" otherwise known as the year 2000 (Y2K) date data problem. Reasonable care requires that an organization take practical and sensible actions to guarantee the fulfillment of their fiduciary responsibilities and the meeting of other legal and business obligations. To demonstrate reasonable care is to provide documentary evidence that reasoned actions have actually been taken to solve a known problem.

From the perspective of societal dependency, the most susceptible systems for causing adverse impacts include:

- Communications, telecommunications, and networks.
- Emergency services, fire, police, ambulance, disaster recovery.
- Energy, generation and supply.
- Finance, banking, and stock market trading.
- Food supply, shipping, storage, and distribution.
- National security, intelligence services, defense, and weapon systems.
- Public health, hospital, pharmaceutical, and medical devices.
- Government treasury, tax collection, customs, excise, property, sales, disbursements, pensions.
- Public assistance, payments.
- Business transactions, supply chains, accounts, payroll, pensions, personnel.
- Transportation, airlines, trains, traffic control, mass transit, shipping, tourism.
- Utilities, water supply, electric, gas, waste disposal.

The critical importance of many computer processing systems, which we take for granted, becomes clear, and society's dependence on these systems, more obvious. Malfunctions in the operations of any of these systems will certainly result in legal action and, perhaps, even future government regulation.

This book outlines the categories and content of documentary evidence that are likely to be needed to demonstrate reasonable care in dealing with the year 2000 date data problem. Further, the book identifies the degree of completion this collection of evidentiary documentation should have attained by the summer and fall of 1998, just one year from the date when massive system failures are likely to occur if left uncorrected— failures that are certain to result in costly lawsuits initiated by stockholders, customers, suppliers, employees, and government agencies seeking recompense for various date data processing-incurred damages. While the form such actions will take is not entirely clear, it is possible to categorize them according to the damages inflicted upon the different originators. For example, stockholders will sue boards of directors and company officials for failure to exercise sound management control over the prevention of date data problem occurrences that have damaged corporate revenue flows and thereby reduced the value of investments and anticipated returns on those investments. Business partners may bring suit for damages incurred through the use of a corporation's faulty products that have damaged their revenue flows or have subjected them to legal actions by their customers. Products may include hard goods that prove untrustworthy due to improper date data handling, such as medical devices, computer software and/or hardware that becomes unreliable due to improper date data processing and communication, and inaccurate or corrupted information due to improper date data processing, storage, and communication to unsuspecting users of the information. Suppliers and creditors may bring action for failure to meet financial obligations due to problems your organization is experiencing in recovering from faulty systems that have interrupted your revenue flows. Employees, likewise, may bring actions for your failure to meet payroll. And finally, government regulatory bodies may be forced to bring actions to curtail operations in dangerous circumstances or recover monetary sums in the form of fines and damages for the general public.

There is a chain of actions that can be triggered by the date data processing problem which has the potential to involve all of your business relationships. At the receiving end of this chain reaction of potential litigation is your entire organization, not just the technology group. While a majority of the documentary evidence required to demonstrate reasonable care will originate from that group, all other elements of the enterprise will be responsible for other key elements such as communications with customers, creditors, and shareholders.

To demonstrate that a reasonable effort was taken in confronting the year 2000 crisis, you must document your efforts. This book helps organizations document that reasonable care was exercised in addressing all enterprise activities and relationships likely to be affected by year 2000 date data processing problems. The goal of such documentation is twofold. First, to show that risk areas associated with date data problems were identified and that actions were taken to prevent and/or mitigate those risks by eliminating the problem in affected systems and by planning contingent actions to keep the business viable while preventing harm to business partners, customers, and third parties. Second, to be ready, if lawsuits are initiated, to show that everything reasonably possible was done to correct the problem and to prevent adverse impacts to others.

Chapter 1 deals with management problems, not just the technical challenges, facing implementors of enterprisewide year 2000 solutions. (Each subsequent chapter will address elements of documentation that serve as evidence of reasonable care.) Chapter 2 identifies the corporate or government agency legal documentation that needs to be assembled to demonstrate officer, director, and executive involvement with the Y2K corrective action program and which outlines the legal and contract obligations under which the enterprise must operate. Chapter 3 discusses those elements of documentation that indicate whether an enterprise is knowledgeable about internal and external date data impacted exchanges of information required for the successful execution of all business-related functions. Chapter 4, addressing one of the most difficult areas in which to assemble documentation, outlines key elements of information about computers/networks/applications software, date data inventories, and systems management activities needed to demonstrate overall knowledge and control of potentially troublesome systems. Without such documentation, it could prove difficult to convince an objective observer that reasonable efforts were taken to prevent year 2000 damages from occurring.

Chapter 5 identifies documentation associated with management of a year 2000 project. Such documents demonstrate the progression of analysis and decisions that went into solutions. This chapter is at the center of being able to demonstrate that reasonable actions were taken to address the year 2000 challenge. Chapter 6 addresses elements of documentation that indicate that system operational concerns have been addressed during the course of implementing year 2000 corrective actions. Finally,

Chapter 7 deals with the issues surrounding the use of microprocessors that are embedded in many production and process control systems as well as facility management and environmental support systems.

The nature of the year 2000 problem (i.e., enterprisewide business impacts) means that it cannot be addressed on a technical level alone. This problem goes to the operating core of most organizations and reveals to many nontechnical executives two far-reaching realities about the use of computers: First, the extent to which technology permeates their business and the attendant risks such a degree of dependence entails; and second, the obvious need to manage future uses of computer technology in a much more disciplined and responsible manner, always focusing on the total business requirement and coordinating all technology decisions at an executive level where technological opportunities can be effectively weighed against a heightened sensitivity to risk. In other words, manage the technology in such a way that another such fiasco cannot occur.

The year 2000 crisis provides us with a forum to address many heretofore ignored information technology problems from the perspective of enterprise dependence and business survivability. For example, a vast majority of organizations do not have accurate inventories of hardware, software, and data assets. The first task called for in most year 2000 statements of work is to conduct an inventory. Many businesses do not keep current inventories of these important assets. Very basic resource management failures regarding information technology are coming to the forefront of executive consciousness after decades of neglect.

Solving the enterprisewide year 2000 problem demands a very detailed accounting for the uses of information technology and this book, as it addresses the documentation issues surrounding reasonable care and business contingency planning, assists executives with this new perspective. It also assists in creating a baseline of information technology resource management data needed to successfully utilize this technology in the twenty-first century. By creating a resource management baseline for year 2000 purposes, this book, with its management review approach, allows corporate, executive, and government officials to ask questions that go beyond the briefing charts and into the heart of responsible asset planning and management.

Read on to discover how you can responsibly prepare your organization to meet this crisis.

TIMOTHY B. BRAITHWAITE

1

THE YEAR 2000 PROBLEM: MANAGING TO DEMONSTRATE REASONABLE CARE

In this chapter, we explore the year 2000 date data problem from a technical project management perspective and identify conditions existing in most information technology organizations that will make the gathering of reasonable care documentation difficult. Several excellent books treat the various year 2000 technical problems and their solutions, but the successful implementation of those technical solutions is influenced by certain realities, founded in the history of information technology and its management. One of the basic reasons for the difficulty many organizations are experiencing is the often-expressed sentiment that "year 2000 solutions are *not* difficult to implement technically." When combined with the seemingly simple nature of the problem—after all how could you not know what year it is—the issue has seemed by many to be blown out of proportion. While the solution, in the abstract, may not be technically challenging, the management of the solution will greatly tax project management capabilities and will require the effective and efficient operation of several overall system management processes and practices, such as configuration management, change control, and testing. These procedures and practices are often missing, ignored, or poorly enforced, having an adverse impact on year 2000 corrective efforts. For most technology-dependent enterprises, who have not experienced an acquisition or a merger, where differing information technology systems must be integrated, there has never been a project of this magnitude.

Let us now explore, in more detail, certain realities of the typical information technology support environment and determine if such conditions are conducive to correcting the year 2000 date data problem and providing the documentary evidence required to show reasonable care (RC).

HARDWARE AND SOFTWARE PRODUCT DEPENDENCIES

The vast majority of information technology support environments are heterogenous to some degree and with diversity comes problems not experienced in a single-vendor shop. Using a single vendor as supplier, the complexity of verifying year 2000 compliance is greatly reduced, since vendor-corrected upgrades will undoubtedly have been tested within the vendor's product line. Environments comprised of multiple vendor products, however, pose a much greater degree of verification complexity since each year 2000 fix will be based on each vendor's proprietary system's design. Fixes will not be released with the customer's implementation schedule in mind, and interoperability testing with other vendor products will not generally have taken place. This means that each enterprise will be required to conduct their own compliance and interoperability testing based on internal configuration needs. If the conditions outlined in the rest of this chapter are even partially true for any of your vendors, then the likelihood for year 2000 confusion and poor coordination is high. Your enterprise must integrate a year 2000 compliant release from *each* vendor into an operational system that can support the requirements of your year 2000 compliant business software applications. This is only one of many such dependencies that will influence the ability of the enterprise to continue to deliver uninterrupted business services to its customers. By the summer and fall of 1998, support vendors of hardware, systems software, and off-the-shelf packages should have communicated clearly their product upgrade plans and schedules for when upgrades will be available for customer integration into their operational configurations. Vendors who have not been forthcoming by that date should be carefully documented and a possible replacement evaluated.

The reality of the contemporary information technology support environment is that a vast number of dependencies exist and all must be year 2000 compliant within the framework of your extended business requirements and relationships. Even with support environments totally outside of the enterprise's control, such as an Internet provider, those responsible for enterprise year 2000 compliance must anticipate the possibility of failure and develop contingency plans. A special caution is called for regarding the Internet and web technology. There has been a tendency among some to speak of using the web as a way around year 2000 problems, as though the Internet were somehow immune. *It is not.* The Internet is comprised of hardware and software subject to the same year 2000 defects as any other system. It is highly advisable that each organization develop relationship and dependency diagrams for *all* support systems with special emphasis on those outside the immediate control of the enterprise. Careful monitoring and documentation of all vendor contacts regarding year 2000 readiness is required.

The identification of system support dependencies is a difficult undertaking in all but the most disciplined shops. Once identified and documented, special care must be taken to keep track of any changes to the configuration to insure that the integrity of a baselined environment is maintained.

DATA INTEGRITY

In a world of rapidly changing technology, with its incessant pressure to upgrade to the next enhancement, it is easy to lose sight of the purpose of an information technology organization. The year 2000 problem, with its inherent threat to data integrity, reminds us that the accurate and timely processing of information is the reason for much of the technology in the first place. Few problems could pose a greater threat to that purpose than the corruption of files brought about through erroneous date data processing. Since accurate information is the lifeblood of business and government decision making, any threat to that information is a threat to the viability of the enterprise. This view is not fully appreciated by many business executives and government officials. Information is often viewed as merely a by-product of some transaction, a recording of an event. Not until information is viewed as representing the reality of an account, an individual, an inventory level, and so on, and computer processing of records are actually seen as altering the reality of each account, individual, inventory level, does the critical importance of data integrity begin to be understood. Faulty date data processing will produce erroneous information that will inaccurately change account, individual, and inventory level, and so forth representations, corrupting heretofore accurate data stores.

Where year 2000 date data processing problems are anticipated, corrected, and tested, processing continues past the year 2000 *without*

compromising data integrity. This is the *best* case. The second best case
is when erroneous date data processing outputs cause the executing software to cease operating before data stores can be corrupted. The third
best case is when erroneous date data processing outputs are caught by an
edit or an audit routine and corrective action can be taken to re-establish
data record accuracy. The *worst* case is when erroneous date data processing outputs don't cause the software to cease operation, aren't caught
by edits or audit routines, and inaccurate outputs replace previously accurate data stores. When undetected, more and more of the data files become corrupted.

It is therefore highly advisable that each organization develop detailed
data flow documentation accounting for all date-related data processing
inputs and outputs entering and exiting a business process and its automated support systems. These date-related data flows should clearly identify inputs from outside the enterprise, outputs leaving the enterprise,
and all date-related data processing output exchanges within the enterprise. The chain of date data dependencies identified by the data flow
documentation is essential for demonstrating that an organization knows
the origins and destinations of potentially troublesome date-related data
so that year 2000 remediation efforts can be targeted to areas of high
risk. Without such documentation, it will be difficult to focus the remediation effort, inform business partners of potential problems, and protect customers from adverse impacts due to information inaccuracies.

There is a domino effect that inaccurate information, triggered by faulty
date data processing, can initiate. Each recipient of inaccurate information
uses that data for some business purpose and may pass it along unchanged
or as part of a new information product to their business partners. Corruption of the data stores of many different enterprises can be extensive, with
each constituting a potential lawsuit. For this reason, lawyers are beginning
to show great interest in the year 2000 issue and its ramifications.

COMPUTING ASSET MANAGEMENT

Two decades of computer processing decentralization have created difficult conditions in which to successfully implement a year 2000 date
data correction program. In many organizations, individual business units
have created their own computer processing and delivery support capabilities with little or no regard for the enterprise as a whole. This has led
to inadequately defined information exchange policies and even more

poorly implemented information systems needed to serve the entire organization. Interoperability problems are common and nonstandard date data coding practices abound. Such systems grew in isolation and have only recently been evolving toward interactive data exchanges. Identifying all data flows and system date-related data exchanges can prove very difficult with decentralized information technology implementations.

SOFTWARE DEVELOPMENT PRACTICES

Initially the year 2000 problem was dismissed as less than technically challenging. It was also determined to be a problem that existed primarily with older COBOL programs or "legacy" systems. A more correct description would be that it is a problem existing with any software, hardware, or firmware system, regardless of when created, where two digits were used to represent the year field of a date. This revised definition provides for a more accurate description of the scope of the problem. It is a problem associated with programming convention and coding practices and, except for the instance where a programming language enforces a four-digit year field rule, we are likely to find two-digit fields being coded into new software even today. While most newer language compilers allow for four-digit year representations, it has been left largely to the discretion of the programmer to implement. Predictably, many older COBOL programs have been simply converted into newer languages while maintaining the original record and field descriptions and formats found in the original COBOL. Unless a conscious design decision to go with a four-digit year field was made and then enforced and tested, there are no assurances that newer applications are not threatened by the same year 2000 problem as the older systems.

Software development is a documentation-intensive undertaking—an undertaking that historically has been poorly performed. In Chapter 4, the essential elements of documentation required to effectively demonstrate management of a portfolio of software application will be identified. Sufficient useable documentation must be available to claim reasonable knowledge and control over the software undergoing remediation.

Additionally, regarding software development, it is generally agreed that testing is usually not adequate, and that "bugs" are an accepted way of life. This has led to the practice of letting the customer do testing by default and report defects back to the developer. This approach has sabotaged attempts to improve quality assurance testing before product release, since it is obviously quicker, cheaper, and apparently acceptable to the vast majority of customers who have been conditioned to expect "bugs." Bad practices are hard to break and it is likely that the current status quo testing model will be unconsciously applied to date change testing. Unfortunately, the year 2000 problem does not allow for a safe period (i.e., after January 1, 2000)* of customer testing. These are production bread-and-butter systems that must run correctly, exchanging accurate date-related data with other systems and with business partners who need accurate data to meet their business obligations. With time getting short, the temptation to treat year 2000 testing as merely "status quo" testing is a sure recipe for disaster. Systems must work correctly on January 1, 2000, or business interruptions will be experienced, and with business interruptions come law suits for recovery of lost revenues and other damages. There is no allowing for the "patch-it-as-we-go" mentality of the past when an average of 7 out of each 100 lines of code contain a reference to a date. All code corrections must be accomplished during the code remediation phase, with completed systems and user acceptance testing being accomplished *before* the application's drop-dead date. This means that the critical path *is* the testing path. Testing must be considered an activity concurrent with remediation. Documentation regarding all aspects of year 2000 testing must be developed and kept current during the entire remediation and test period. This will prove difficult in environments where testing has never been institutionalized with enforced policies, standards, practices, and procedures.

SYSTEM MANAGEMENT PRACTICES

As noted in the preface, many organizations have experienced difficulty getting their year 2000 remediation efforts underway because they lack accurate inventories and descriptions of their computer hardware, software, data, and communication system components. This inability to account for capital assets is not conceivable with other areas of business and yet it has been tolerated or never required of the various information technology groups.

Many reasons for this lapse of good management practices stem from the way in which automation support has evolved. Initially, computers and software were considered to be rather esoteric and part of the world

---

* Or whatever the drop-dead date may be for a given application.

of research and development, or a tool of the mathematics department. Computers were scarce, expensive, and tightly controlled by a few persons. Later, as computers were applied to business record keeping and transaction processing, the centralized mainframe department was established, but again, the hardware and software was physically located in a few locations under the control of specially trained personnel. In this environment, however, the first problems with systems management and control began to surface. These problems were related primarily to the controls over software that are required if an organization desires not to be held hostage by a programmer.

To prevent this undesirable situation from developing, good system management practices held that software should be created in a structured and disciplined fashion, using techniques borrowed from the world of engineering. These structured techniques followed the problem-solving process associated with complex engineering tasks (i.e., requirement/problem definition, solution exploration, solution design, programming, testing, and implementation/maintenance) and required detailed documentation of each step of the process. In this way, software could be formulated in a more scientific and repeatable manner and could be more easily understood by other programmers, thus reducing the risk of a single programmer being the only person understanding a piece of software that an organization depended on for a critical business function.

Many different structured techniques have evolved, over the last 20 years, into software engineering approaches that do, in part, overcome the risks posed by the lone "arts-and-crafts" programmer. There is one major weakness, however, with the engineering approach to software development—such practices must be *expected* and *enforced* by management. Validation and verification that software engineering practices have been followed is a systems management function that all too often has not been performed. Without enforcement, the use of engineering techniques during software development is left to the discretion of the individual programmer, and in the usual haste to meet deadlines, these techniques are seldom used rigorously. Documentation is generally the first engineering requirement to suffer on most software development projects, and yet it is through documentation that the analytic process required by software engineering is communicated to others. Without documentation, the thought process that went into the software is unknown, and without documentation, the level of knowledge required to demonstrate reasonable care cannot be established.

Additionally, in the centralized mainframe environment, other system management problems began to surface, including the ability to keep track of the myriad equipments that began to be connected to the mainframe by both hardwire and dial-up communications. Inventory systems were installed and monitored. In organizations where sensitive data were processed by computer, these control systems were essential to establishing even the most basic security. Configuration management systems, a step up from just keeping accurate inventories, were soon implemented to account for all hardware and software assets and, when used in conjunction with capacity utilization tools, to forecast future system capacity requirements before existing system resources were exhausted. Changes to production software also became problematic, and change control systems and version release management controls were established. These system management techniques subjected software changes to the same discipline that systems engineering afforded new development efforts. Without such system management controls, it was virtually impossible to know what equipment and users were connected to a computer system, what software was resident on the system, and whether or not the software had been properly developed and tested before being allowed to influence the integrity of all other operating software. Again such controls had to be enforced, but it was generally recognized by management that overall system stability and reliability depended upon such controls. By the late 1970s, centralized mainframe environments could at least account for their computing assets and had some form of configuration management and change control in place.

Enter the personal computer and the quickly evolving technologies that have allowed entire computer processing departments to be created overnight, generally beyond the management control philosophy of the centralized mainframe group. The explosion that followed has resulted in the common enterprise situation, where multiple vendors running proprietary software systems that process corporate data that is nonstandard can't communicate with each other. Furthermore, the rapid growth of nonmainframe computing has outstripped the supply of professional systems people, leading to the high turnover rate of an employee's market.

From a systems management perspective, techniques such as configuration management, software change control, and version release management have been slow to be embraced. Such techniques weren't needed in the early "stand alone" phase of most systems. It has only been in the last five years, since stand alones began to be integrated into enterprisewide configurations, that such techniques became applicable. By then, the problems of configuration and software incompatibilities were so great, and the management tools so immature, that progress in establishing system management controls was difficult to achieve. This has been especially true where large quantities of end user-developed software are used throughout the enterprise.

All of these problems with system management practices conspire to make it difficult to be able to demonstrate that the many system assets likely to be impacted by the year 2000 problem were under the degree of control necessary to effectuate corrective action. It will be hard to convince others that reasonable care was exercised if the enterprise can't point to accurate inventories and system controls that were in place to account for and document changes. How can you claim to have *it* under control if you don't even know what or where *it* is?

STATE OF QUALITY

The old adage "we never have time to do it right—but we always have time to do it again," has become an accepted way of doing business in the world of IT. This attitude will spell disaster with regards to the year 2000 problem. The "time to do it again" is *now* and there is a firm deadline. We got into this predicament because the industry continued to put off the fix for over 20 years—there was always "time to do it again."

What other circumstances have intentionally and unintentionally contributed to make "doing it right" so difficult? The following conditions are sure to influence the effectiveness of a year 2000 corrective action program and should result in mitigation plans to assure that activities to support a defense of reasonable care are in fact performed:

1. The degree of complexity that is commonplace to most information processing environments is not understood and appreciated by nontechnical decision makers. This is especially true where commercial off-the-shelf (COTS) hardware and software products form the underlying foundation for a special purpose systems solution. COTS, by its very nature, is supposed to solve the problems of building systems, not create difficulties because of incompatibilities. COTS is usually sold as an 80 percent solution as though the remaining 20 percent weren't significant. Experience indicates otherwise.

From a hardware perspective, we must remember that the experience of most managers arises from the desktop, stand alone PC application. Complexity has increased as the desire to share information through networked PCs has grown. But the ability to manage those networks has lagged far behind the desire, with the result that systems don't materialize at anywhere near the projected costs or in the time estimated.

2. Potential (i.e., meaning it worked in a laboratory environment) information technologies are written about and marketed as though they were commonplace, even though they are not fully developed and certainly not tested in a workplace atmosphere. The term vaporware has been used by some to describe these potential products. Since performance cost and time estimated to implement vaporware are based on a fantasy (i.e., that the technology works), management's expectations, following a decision to use the technology, can never be realistic. The end result is that executive business plans and promises concerning the enterprises' use of the technology are often based on the same fantasy.

3. Over-promising and the use of vague success criteria should be expected from the world of marketing, particularly in a new industry where few benchmarks exist and where companies come and go with great frequency.

4. Due to the volatility of the IT industry, one would think that great caution would prevail when selecting underlying technologies and system strategies. Yet the only *risk* that seems to get attention is the *risk* of *not moving quickly* to adopt and adapt to new architectures, software, and systems. When faced with aggressive marketing techniques constructed around the "don't be left behind" argument and the benefit studies showing the shopworn "reduction in hardware costs curve" while being uncomfortably imprecise about software costs and network expenses, it is difficult to *not throw caution* to the wind and get on the bandwagon! Without a counteracting risk to the business analysis, everyone knows enough to be a cheerleader.

5. IT careers depend on being at the cutting edge of new technologies. In early 1997, skills with client/server systems design and object-oriented programming demanded salaries two to three times that of a COBOL programmer working with mainframe systems. This imbalance speaks to the disdain with which older technologies and their practitioners are held, even though the older technologies (i.e., mainframe and COBOL) are where the "bread-and-butter" processing still takes place. Due to the year 2000 problem, COBOL programmers can now demand salaries in excess of those paid to new technology practitioners—an interesting turn of events!

6. Open system standards aren't fully adhered to! While boasting compliance with open standards, vendors still secretly devise ways, usually in product implementation of a standard, to get customers hooked into their proprietary systems solution. If standards were truly followed, most incompatibilities between various vendors would not exist. But, they do exist, and it is difficult to know, ahead of time, what problem and delays will be encountered because of them. Nontechnical decision makers often take the claims of open system adherence as gospel, and are later shocked to hear that components from different "open" suppliers are experiencing interface difficulties.

7. Project estimates always fall short, driven as they are by the generally optimistic nature of technologists and the experience of a management that has grown accustomed to "heroic" efforts to bring a project to completion. Gambling continued corporate revenues and reputation on heroics, however, is a very questionable way to run a year 2000 project. Just because some employees were willing to risk burnout on the last several projects doesn't mean they will sign up for another mismanaged effort requiring more of the same. And believe it, they know when a project is mismanaged.

In summary, each of these conditions and realities conspire to throw any IT project into crisis. Since estimates concerning the time to "do it right" are not believed to be valid, quality assurance and testing get sacrificed as the immovable project deadline draws near. And since executive management has no clear understanding of what it really costs to field an inadequately tested product, past practices continue to be the prologue to the future. Except, the future is now and with the year 2000 problem, mistakes made over the last 40 years are going to make a difficult problem even worse.

INCREASING WORKLOADS WHILE DOWNSIZING STAFF

While most information technology staffs have escaped official reductions in force, many have had to absorb an ever-increasing backlog of development and integration requirements brought about through corporate mergers and acquisitions. As is often the case, none of the acquired company's system applications, development tools, and languages or equipment architectures are compatible with anything the gaining IT staff has experience with.

At the same time, many of the restructuring business efficiencies promised by such mergers and acquisitions are based on the elimination of some duplicate computer systems while other systems must pick up the lost productivity experienced following forced retirements and lay-offs. More work, greater incompatibilities, increased complexities, and raised management and shareholder expectations conspire to shorten delivery times and put tremendous pressures on the existing development staff, with software quality and business performance hanging in the balance. Add the pressure of year 2000 remediation efforts and you have conditions ripe for staff meltdowns and defections.

LACK OF TESTING AND EXPERIENCED TESTERS

Dr. Vern J. Crandall, formerly of Brigham Young University and a noted expert on testing and the software development industry, has made some very interesting observations. According to Dr. Crandall, "It is amazing that in this period of pervasive software development, there are a great many organizations that do not have independent test organizations. Indeed, some very well-known companies do not do testing at all!" Dr. Crandall goes on to point out the economic shortsightedness of such neglect. "[T]hink of a product with 1 million users. Suppose a serious flaw is found in the product after it has been shipped, one that would cause catastrophic data loss to a user. If one has a list of customers and one copies a diskette containing the fix (assuming that the customer can install the new software with little difficulty), and assume that it costs $10.00 to copy the diskette and mail it to the customer, that single error has cost the company $10 million!"* One company refused to pay the price of an independent test unit until one error caused a major product recall and cost them $500,000, not to mention loss of reputation. That $500,000 could have paid for a lot of testing and saved a blow to their corporate reputation.

Why the reluctance to test? Why the failure to learn from the misfortune of others in the software business? Aside from the obvious denial that is going on, a possible reason lies in the fact that staffing a competent test organization is by no means easy. Again, according to Dr. Crandall,

---

* Vern Crandall, PhD, *How to Reduce the Software Development Life Cycle,* Provo, UT: Brigham Young University, 21, 1991.

"[I]n the University environment, there are fewer than ten software testing courses in the United States of which the author is aware—and most of these are theoretical." Also, testing is generally viewed as a lesser job than programming, and management's reluctance to pay testers as well as programmers supports this view. Testing is often seen as a part-time job, sometimes shared with trouble-desk duties. Neither position is glamorous or thought of as creative, and if career advancement is desired, both positions are best ignored, by-passed, or moved through quickly. These attitudes certainly can't make year 2000 testing any easier.

PROCESS AND DOCUMENTATION
CAUTIONARY NOTE

A side benefit of watching the O.J. Simpson trial marathon was the insight that the execution of any process or procedure can be questioned to the point that doubt can be raised as to the validity of the work products exiting the process. The procedures in this instance dealt with investigative routines followed by the Los Angeles Police Department and Coroner's Office, while the processes dealt with everything from processing a crime scene to the laboratory processes for arriving at blood type and DNA conclusions. It was fascinating to watch the defense's deliberate strategy of first establishing the fact that standard investigative and evidence processing procedures exist, that the text books and curriculum describe and teach these procedures, and that the witness-practitioners were fully aware of such procedures and even supervised their application. Then, to observe the ease with which each investigative and evidence processing conclusion could be called into question caused me to pause and reflect upon a similar strategy whereby charges of year 2000 computer system and software liability could be alleged and substantiated. And further, if a rational argument could establish and support such an allegation, then a set of rational preventative actions to negate such allegations could be defined and formulated. In other words, this rationale could be utilized, as a guide, by those wishing to bring a charge of year 2000 liability and by those software developers and system integrators wishing to lessen their risk of succumbing to such charges of liability.

To be sure, there is a difference between raising the spectre of doubt in a criminal case and proving that an organization did not exercise reasonable care with regard to the year 2000 problem. But, the strategy of raising doubt about the efficacy of the processes and practices used to address the year 2000 problem is valid. This approach is successfully used in cases of medical liability and with all other disciplines that are guided by accepted and expected ways of doing business. A standard is established as a prevailing method being followed in accomplishing a task and then adherence to, or deviations from, the standard are established for the case under consideration. Judgments are then made concerning whether the deviations caused the problem complained of, with liability being determined.

Earlier it was stressed that documentation was the key to a reasonable care defense. It must now be recognized that documentation means not only the execution of a statement that an action was taken, but that the work by-product of the action itself must often constitute the evidence that the action was taken. For example, an audit review item receiving an affirmative check-off, such as "Were data flow diagrams used to determine the destinations of data exiting a program module?" would be accompanied by the data flow diagrams themselves, thus providing evidence that the action was actually taken. In this case, the data flow diagram is the by-product of an analysis to determine the destination of a data item exiting a program's execution. While this may seem obvious to most, it is an area that can lead to problems in an IT organization. It is often the practice to require development and operations level officials and personnel to certify that certain analytic studies have taken place before approvals can be given to proceed with a technology project. Unless such studies are actually reviewed by oversight groups, they quickly become pro forma "paper drills" or aren't completed at all—merely checked off.

Chapters 2 through 7 will identify more elements of information needed to be able to demonstrate reasonable care. This is not a checklist, not a pro forma paper drill. Real analysis will be required for each element with real documentation reflecting how that analysis developed. Anything less could well be indefensible.

2

REASONABLE CARE: CORPORATE/AGENCY LEGAL DOCUMENTATION REQUIREMENTS

This is the first of six chapters that will suggest the actions that any enterprise, be it corporate or governmental, should be able to show occurred while addressing the year 2000 problem. In describing such actions, and the documentary evidence to show that such actions occurred, the following definitions apply and provide a rationale for the actions:

- *Reasonable care:* That degree of care which a person of ordinary prudence would exercise in the same or similar circumstances. Due care under all the circumstances. Failure to exercise such care is ordinary negligence *(Black's Law Dictionary)*.
- *Due diligence:* The degree of effort and care in carrying out an act or obligation that the average, sincere, energetic person would exhibit; conduct that is devoid of negligence or carelessness *(The Plain-Language Law Dictionary,* Robert Rothenberg, Penguin 1981).
- *Negligence:* Failure to do what a reasonable and prudent person would ordinarily have done under the circumstances of the situation, or doing what such a person would not have done. Involves a breach of duty toward the person complaining *(Anderson's Law Dictionary)*.
- *Contributory negligence:* The absence of reasonable care and caution in a given case, on the part of the complainant *(Anderson's Law Dictionary)*.

Appendix A, Vendor Liability and the Year 2000 Crisis, presents some of the legal pitfalls found in crossing these uncharted liability waters and how they can be recognized and avoided. This research bulletin outlines the potential liability of vendors, including year 2000 service providers.

Underlying a response for each exposure, especially in cases where the risk was known, is the need to demonstrate, through documentary evidence, that care and diligence were taken. The documentation trail, while heavily based on technology activities (i.e., Chapters 4, 5, and 6) actually begins at the highest executive levels of the enterprise where overall direction and year 2000 priorities must be established.

PREVAILING STATUTES, REGULATIONS, AND DISCLOSURE REQUIREMENTS

As a director, or other highly placed official, of a corporation or government agency, you must be able to show that you were familiar with the potential problems posed by the year 2000 challenge—that if left uncorrected, many computers, computer programs, and embedded-chip devices will perform as though the new year 00 is 1900 and not 2000. Your customers, investors, and business partners expect that you will take measures to prevent disruptions of normal business activities that will put them, their investment, or their business at risk. They expect adherence to what your regulators have directed. For example, in 1996 the U.S. Controller of the Currency told all National Bank CEOs to complete year 2000 compliance by December 31, 1998; in 1997, the U.S. Senate Banking Committee imposed a December 1998 compliance requirement on the Federal Reserve Bank and its subsidiaries. Further, for corporations, Security and Exchange Commission (SEC) Regulation S-K, Item 303, requires that the annual 10K statement's "Discussion and Analysis" of your financial condition and operations contain "matters that would have impact on future operations and have not had an impact in the past." In other words, shareholders should be informed about corporate year 2000 exposures, what is being done to correct them, and what impacts they may have on future business revenues.

For those regulated by the Food and Drug Administration (FDA), specific announcements have been published to ensure continued safety and effectiveness of computer systems, software, and embedded

microprocessors used in medical devices. The following actions are recommended by the Office of Device Evaluation: Food and Drug Administration, in a document entitled "Deciding When to Submit a Form
510(k)":

—For *future* medical device premarket submissions, manufacturers
should assure that the products can perform date recording and compu-
tations that will be unaffected by the year 2000 date change.

—For *currently manufactured* medical devices, manufacturers should
conduct hazard and safety analyses to determine whether service performance could be affected by the year 2000-date change. If these analyses show that device safety or effectiveness could be affected, then
appropriate steps should be taken to correct current production and to assist customers who have purchased such devices.

—For computer-controlled *design, production and quality control
processes,* manufacturers should assure the two-digit date formats or com-
putations do not cause problems beginning January 1, 2000.

Manufacturers should also note that under the previous GMP [Good Manufacturing Practices] regulation and the current Quality System Regulation, effective June 1, 1997, they must investigate and correct problems
with medical devices that present a significant risk to public health. This
includes devices that fail to operate according to their specifications because of inaccurate date recording and/or calculations. Section 518 of
the Food, Drug and Cosmetic Act requires notification of users or purchasers when a device presents an unreasonable risk of substantial harm
or public health.

For federal government agencies, a seldom enforced law, Pub. Law
No. (PL) 93-579, The Privacy Act of 1974, prescribes certain conditions,
regarding recording keeping and data kept on citizens, where civil action
can be brought for damages against the government. The conditions include the willful use of inaccurate information about a citizen that results in an adverse action or consequence affecting the individual.
Government agencies that fail to demonstrate reasonable care in correcting their year 2000 problems may find increased interest in PL 93-
579 on the part of citizens and lawyers alike.

Whatever line of business the enterprise is pursuing or whatever the
law or government program being administered, prevailing laws, regulations, and statutes must be identified and scrutinized for requirements
that direct or imply the accurate processing of dates and date-related

information. These requirements provide the legal foundation for all subsequent year 2000 decisions and prioritization of actions.

RISK ANALYSIS: SET PRIORITIES AND
IDENTIFY ALL IMPACTED PARTIES

Solutions for correcting the year 2000 problem will require substantial resources and the careful allocation of those scarce resources to the correction of systems likely to adversely impact the continued viability of the business if not corrected. Successful completion of a risk analysis requires both a business and technical understanding of threats to the enterprise's conduct of core business functions and the threat the enterprise poses to customers, business partners, and citizens through failure to correct high impact systems. The completion of such a risk analysis requires an in-depth understanding of business processes and date-data uses and exchanges with those inside and outside the organization. This in-depth knowledge is supported by many of the analyses and documents to be outlined in Chapters 3 through 6 and by mini-risk assessments done throughout the organization as the year 2000 corrective program unfolds. It is incumbent on the leadership to be able to identify that conscious risk decisions were made to take one particular course of corrective action over another. A risk analysis is not accomplished to prove whether a course of action was right or wrong, effective or ineffective, only that year 2000 actions were consciously determined after careful consideration of identified risk factors. The process of year 2000 risk management is an *iterative* process of "bottom-up, top-down" deliberations to identify risks, select corrective actions within a priority scheme, implement corrective actions, evaluate actions, and reassess those risks that are now present within the decreasing time frame. The exercise of risk management will be a continuous activity of executive leadership with documentation recording all deliberations and decisions.

PREPARE FOR DIRECTORS AND OFFICERS
TO BE PERSONALLY LIABLE

Can corporate directors and officers be held personally liable for failures and damages resulting from their business's lack or ineffective response to technology problems? Generally, directors and officers have limited personal liability to third parties. However, a director or officer who breaches his duties of good faith, fair dealing, and/or due care may find himself liable to the corporation itself, through a shareholder's derivative lawsuit. All directors are required to exercise reasonable diligence and care in the process of making informed decisions. Generally speaking, if the year 2000 problem were a surprise to your directors and to your competition and the general population as well, they would not be liable. However, given the amount of publicity this problem has received, it would seem foolhardy to mount a defense based on surprise and claim ignorance of the problem. In such instances, directors may be held personally liable to the corporation's shareholders for failures to make informed decisions when plenty of information concerning the problem existed and warnings were being given—sometimes in the form of government regulations.

DIRECTOR'S AND OFFICER'S INSURANCE

Director's and officer's (D&O) insurance protects these officials in instances of normal human fallibility. Your insurance carrier can clarify specific coverage questions with regard to year 2000 issues. Very often, however, these policies carry exclusions for intentional acts, and sometimes even for reckless or grossly negligent acts. Therefore, since the criteria to be met in order for insurance coverage to apply is to exercise reasonable diligence and care—making informed decisions—the documentation trail outlined in this book will help to show that the D&Os took reasonable measures, and even if such decisions were wrong (i.e., they were fallible), the D&Os were exercising their management functions and prerogatives—they weren't intentionally or recklessly ignoring the issue, hoping it would go away. Summarized, D&Os should be able to show that they:

- Established a year 2000 project and provided funding;
- Inventoried all business and computerized systems, and all date data exchanges of information and all third party dependencies;
- Performed a risk assessment and developed a plan of action;
- Used outside resources appropriately; and

- Tracked progress and reported honestly to employees, customers, investors, business partners, and government regulators.

DOCUMENT DELIBERATIONS AND DECISIONS TO DEMONSTRATE REASONABLE CARE

If the enterprise is a member of an industry where "best practices" have evolved, it is advisable to be able to demonstrate adherence to those practices. Anyone attempting to bring into question your year 2000 practices will almost certainly examine the extent to which your management system is already in order vis-à-vis any industry standard or de facto standard practices. For example, if it is standard practice to employ a structured analysis, design, and programming approach for the development of software, and your company doesn't, the failure to have followed the standard may be presented as evidence that care and diligence were not taken in software development. Furthermore, since the structured underpinnings of good software will be shown to be missing, the efficacy and adequacy of year 2000 corrective actions will immediately be called into question. Only comprehensive testing will be able to overcome the impressions of a lackadaisical attitude toward software development.

Documents that indicate executive establishment and pro-active involvement in the year 2000 solution need to be formalized and available for critics of your efforts. Additionally, evidence of progress reviews and periodic executive status report sessions indicate management's understanding of the serious nature of the problem and the need for their oversight. The legal implications of any course of action need to be reviewed by appropriate individuals with formal evaluations being presented to the officers and board of directors.

The Gartner Group has made studied estimates concerning the worldwide cost of fixing the year 2000 problem and have set the amount at approximately two-thirds of a trillion dollars. Whatever the final amount only time will tell, but enterprise executives need to be able to carefully document the dollar amount needed to insulate their information systems and all potentially impacted parties from date data vulnerabilities. Since the costs are high, difficult decisions will be called for. The very fact that such decisions were made indicates the degree of seriousness attributed to the problem by executive management. For example, only the most severe problem would cause the redirection of resources from "value-added" new technology initiatives to a nonvalue-added fix-it project. The

U.S. Army for instance, lacking the necessary incremental funds, immediately shut down information systems considered to be nonessential and re-deployed their resources to year 2000 corrective efforts. Additionally, the Army halted all new development on remaining applications, except for production emergencies, until after they are all year 2000 ready. Put another way, only the most prosperous companies will be able to continue business as usual while addressing the year 2000 problem. For most organizations, after failures have occurred and damages been experienced, to be perceived as having had a business-as-usual attitude can only be seen as evidence that the problem was not taken seriously and that diligence and care were not practiced. Drastic challenges call for drastic measures and will be viewed as a necessary level of commitment.

Documentation—recording each attempt to communicate to all interested parties the impacts of year 2000 problems—should be carefully compiled. The principal output for the previously discussed risk management analysis was the identification of business areas where year 2000 problems could result in an adverse impact, not only for the company, but for customers, creditors, investors, suppliers, citizens, and any other third party. Once identified and once it becomes clear that adverse impacts can't be averted through corrective or contingent actions, each adversely affected entity should be informed in enough time so that they can take individual corrective actions of their own choice. All communications of this nature need to be compiled and kept as evidence that the enterprise intended to deal in "good faith" throughout the period of time that it took to resolve the year 2000 problem and its impacts. Finally, records of independent year 2000 reviews and audits need to be kept as evidence that all reasonable measures (i.e., use of outside expert consultations) were taken to protect the interests of all concerned.

3

CORPORATE/AGENCY INTERNAL AND EXTERNAL DATE DATA EXCHANGE DOCUMENTATION

In Chapter 2, it was discussed that the process of year 2000 risk management was, by its nature, a process of bottom-up, top-down deliberations to identify risks, select corrective actions within a priority scheme, implement corrective actions, evaluate those actions, and finally identify/reassess those risks that are now present due to the decreasing time frame. The top-down decision-making element of this process is dependent on a great deal of information existing at the bottom or operational levels of the enterprise. There are volumes of information concerning date-related data that bear directly on successful remediation efforts and on the requirement for reasonable care documentation. Without information that describes date data origins, processing, retention, usage, destinations, and final disposition, it becomes impossible to make many of the business and technical year 2000 decisions that must be made. Without a good grasp of the date-related data used by the enterprise's many applications, it will also be difficult to show that reasonable care could have been exercised during attempts to correct the problem.

We will now explore some of the information about date data that needs to exist for a successful year 2000 effort and a reasonable care claim.

DATA DICTIONARY AND REPOSITORY RECORDS

Most computerized applications transform data captured from business activities into information used to make business decisions, account for assets, provide services to others, control production processes, or administer business or government programs. In each instance, software manipulates data to achieve the purpose of the system. To do these manipulations, software logic is designed to take a defined data value through a predetermined process. For such programmed logic to work reliably, it must receive as input a dependable standard representation of the data value each and every time. These representations are spelled out in data element definitions and prescribe the length, composition (i.e., alpha, numeric, or alpha numeric), content and allowable values for the data element to be considered valid. All of this information about a data element is required to write a program that accepts and uses or rejects any value that may ever be input as that element. This level of specificity is required for all data elements and are to be found as part of a data dictionary within a repository of overall systems documentation. Information of this type needs to exist for all date data used by any software supporting the enterprise. These descriptions are required for searches through program code to locate occurrences of date references to be corrected.

DATE DATA INTERCHANGES

Also of critical importance is documentation that identifies all of the exchanges of date data between programs making up an application and transfers of date-related information between application systems across the enterprise. Since applications and supporting software have often been developed on different hardware systems using different languages, there will be compatibility problems affecting the exchange of date data that will have to be resolved. Organizations involved in acquisitions and mergers, especially those occurring the last couple of years, are likely to experience this problem to a bewildering degree. Each of these incompatibilities must first be resolved before year 2000 date data exchanges can be solved. In the interim, software will have to be written that translates date data exchanges between systems. This approach, however, still requires complete documentation of the date standards used in each separate system and all exchanges between applications both within the enterprise and external to it. Exchanges of date data between an enterprise and external groups may number into the hundreds, with each representing a point at which database corruption can occur. A reasonable care defense must be able to substantiate that each exchange of date data was known and documented to a degree that technical corrective actions could be taken; and that if time became short or difficulties were encountered, each partner to the exchange was informed of the delay in time to take contingent action.

INFORMATION FLOW RECORDS

The best way to be able to demonstrate knowledge of, and control over, the vast number of date data exchanges experienced by the typical enterprises is to be able to produce documentation showing the flow of information between all systems of the organization. These high-level representations of the business process concentrate on the flows of information affecting those processes. Many organizations have spent a great deal of time and money over the last decade on business process reengineering (BPR) efforts and the type of information flow data needed to show reasonable care is usually a product of such efforts. If a BPR project was conducted in your organization's recent past, information flow documentation should already exist. If it has been kept updated, it should prove valuable.

SECURITY, PRIVACY, AND AUDIT CONTROLS

During implementation of a year 2000 corrective action program, processing systems will be disassembled into workable units of programs and code. These units, perhaps a million lines or so, will be examined by tools and personnel to determine where corrective actions are needed. Likewise, files and databases will be examined to determine where date fields need to be expanded or otherwise manipulated to effect a year 2000 compliance. In either case, software code and file data will be open to close examination and manipulation by personnel, some of whom may not be your own employees. It is important to be able to demonstrate, as part of reasonable care, that proper precautions were taken by management to prevent any breaches of privacy/confidentiality and/or information sensitivity/security controls. This means that adequate controls, preyear 2000 crisis, existed and were enforced so that sufficient short-term contingent controls could be defined, put into place, and enforced during a period of great stress and confusion. For systems under remediation, where stringent accounting and audit rules prevail, the same concern exists. Special before-and-after validation processes may need to be incorporated into later remediation and test procedures to ensure that nothing has been tampered with or compromised. Additionally, many accounting and audit controls exist to ensure the quality and accuracy of data processing and information files. Care must be taken during the remediation process that controls were not accidentally or deliberately disabled in order to meet a date compliance project milestone. The principal defense against this sort of occurrence is two-fold: first, the active participation by the audit and control staff in the year 2000 resolution; and second, comprehensive testing, to include regression testing and systems testing, to ensure that all controls are still in place and properly functioning. We will discuss this in more detail in Chapter 4.

SENIOR EXECUTIVES AND REASONABLE CARE

This chapter and Chapter 2 have dealt with the year 2000 documentation issues that are within areas of direct and immediate concern to senior executives of the enterprise. Both chapters deal with topics that directors and officers should already be dealing with on a day-to-day basis.

Chapter 2 addressed the legal regulatory environment within which the business exists and is allowed to operate. If the executives of the enterprise aren't concerning themselves with these issues, then who is? In truth, no one else is empowered to do so. All that is needed at this level to show reasonable care, assuming that the supporting activities and documents outlined in Chapters 3 through 7 are accomplished, is to demonstrate that management did indeed take the year 2000 problem into consideration during decision making and that they acted in good faith toward all concerned—stockholders, creditors, employees, customers, regulators, citizens, and other third parties.

Chapter 3 issues are also within the direct province of directors and officers, although it is not always as clearly recognized. Chapter 3 addressed the life-blood of the modern business, the management of information. In this age of the information superhighway, when billions of dollars are spent annually on the tools of information processing, what group of senior executives would admit not being cognizant of how information is managed and controlled, who it is shared with, and the risks to their own business or to any of their business partners resulting from corrupted data? To be sure, there will be those at the director level who will claim that such matters are the responsibility of the mid-level managers and the computer technicians; but such an allegation is to admit to a lack of supervision over matters directly influencing the core processes of most modern enterprises. Such allegations will certainly not support a reasonable care defense or find favor with stockholders.

The remaining chapters address the more technical areas of the year 2000 problem for which documentation will also be needed to demonstrate reasonable care. While these issues may not be within the technical competence of the directors and officers, it is still their responsibility to assure stockholders and others that these technical aspects have in fact been accomplished and are sufficient for the continued viability of the business. Executives then, like those outside the enterprise, must also look for evidence that year 2000 corrective actions have been taken. In such cases, executives, in addition to using independent validation techniques and consultants, must primarily look to documentation for assurances that all reasonable actions were taken.

4

COMPUTER/NETWORK/ SOFTWARE/DATABASE AND SYSTEMS DOCUMENTATION

In the Preface, we pointed out that while the year 2000 doesn't require an overly challenging technical solution, it does pose an extremely difficult management problem for most organizations. Most managers don't know how their computerized systems, upon which they so greatly depend, actually work. This lack of knowledge has grown over the years as systems have evolved and new applications have been added to the corporate inventories. Processing environments have extended far beyond the traditional centralized computer complex into decentralized implementations built around specific business units and tied together through communication networks. Desktop computing capabilities have expanded systems operations even deeper into the organization.

Little of this dispersal of physical computing assets, at least during the mid- to late 1980s, was accomplished with any overall plan in mind except to use automation to reduce operating expenses and provide a competitive advantage. What resulted in many enterprises was the uncoordinated acquisition of hardware, software, and communications systems as each business unit did its own thing. Stabilized core administrative functions often stayed at the computer center, but this too has been eventually compromised by compatibility problems with business unit systems, as separate accounting systems began to be viewed as corporatewide resources to be merged and interrogated to make the enterprise more competitive. The average company has the following numbers of separate hardware systems, operating systems, and networks in their computing infrastructure:

Operating systems	5
Nonoperating systems	3–4
Databases	8
Client/server languages	3–4
System network managers	4
Financial-human resource systems	3–4

The significance of this proliferation of heterogenous systems within the enterprise is three-fold:

1. Most processing environments are year 2000 suspect and must be shown to be compliant.
2. Since standardization of business data representation and exchanges is unlikely, each system, even though year 2000 compliant in its own right, must consider each other system as a source of potential date data contamination.
3. Since the information technology industry is suffering the worst skills shortage in its history, it is safe to assume that the processing environment has a skills shortage as well and that these systems are vulnerable to personnel disruptions.

These reasons point to the absolute necessity of having complete and accurate systems documentation, not only for demonstrating reasonable care regarding year 2000 legal challenges, but also for insuring the ability of the enterprise to keep its systems operating and thereby stay in business.

STANDARDS: COMPATIBILITY, INTEROPERABILITY, AND DATE DATA

A reasonable care defense must be able to show that care and diligence were exercised in dealing with the year 2000 problem. This argument of reasonableness, however, needs to show that acting reasonable was possible. It would seem difficult to demonstrate reasonableness in solving this one specific problem if the foundations for routine reasonable action were not evident. In other words, how could reasonable decisions concerning year 2000 actions be argued if documentary evidence concerning inputs to the year 2000 decision process can't be produced? For example, how can a claim that everything was done to inform customers of potential problems with date data coming from our systems be proven, if we don't have documentation substantiating that we know the destination of all system outputs and have a process for identifying new recipients of data as systems are modified or enhanced? If reasonableness in day-to-day management of expensive computing assets and critical corporate information can't be demonstrated, who can believe the sudden reasonableness of solving this particular problem? It is one thing to claim reasonable action and another to show evidence of reasonableness when the underpinnings of reasonable and prudent management are not apparent.

Standards that are defined and enforced for the purpose of producing quality information processing systems and products go a long way toward demonstrating reasonable controls over the systems environment of the enterprise. At the highest level would be organizations that have been actively involved in adopting the International Standards Organization's (ISO 9000) quality standards governing the data-processing industry. These standards have focused on the processes by which systems are defined, designed, developed, tested, and put into production. The quality improvement movement of the past decade has focused on process, not product, in the belief that if the process used to build a product demands that quality be addressed, the final product will likely possess the attributes of quality. So, information technology departments that have been pursuing the ISO standards, and others, such as those prescribed by the American National Standard Institute, the National Institute of Standards and Technology, the Good Manufacturing Practices of the Food and Drug Administration, and the Software Engineering Institute should be in an excellent position to demonstrate the underlying systems management controls needed to support the claim that reasonable decisions and actions are the norm for their organization.

Whether or not such standards are actually followed is another issue and can be determined by requesting documentary evidence and performing spot checks and verifications for quality indicators of a system under development.

PROCESS DOCUMENTATION AND
A MANAGED ENVIRONMENT

The standards programs just cited collectively prescribe a number of quality-enhancing activities and process controls that should be in place and enforced for an information technology environment to be considered well managed. Those activities that have a direct bearing on year 2000 conversion success and for which documentary evidence may be sought will be discussed in the remainder of this chapter. Those activities are necessary because if they are not present, reasonableness will be harder to demonstrate due to the fact that when these activities are not performed, the systems environment tends to get out of control. The truth of this statement will become clear as we examine each activity and control.

STANDARD DATA ELEMENTS AND CODES

Enterprises that don't define and enforce standard data elements and code representations across business units are not only wasteful of information technology resources but are also running the risk of inadvertent contamination of data stores by an unedited nonstandard data element value. If a program policy of using only standard data element names and code representations exists across the enterprise, then it is reasonable to assume that date data is under control and is not likely to pose a significant problem. If, however, standard data element names and code representations are not policy, then it is safe to assume that a lot of data translation is required between systems, that it is apparently acceptable to management for there to be an unnecessary level of data management complexity waiting to compromise file integrity, and finally that any new programmer is allowed to create any data standard within his or her area of responsibility. This situation does not lead one to the conclusion that date data is under control nor likely to be until an overall policy is established and enforced.

The critical point of this example is the need to demonstrate that controls on the content and quality of the data stores exist as a normal course of managing the enterprise's information assets; not that controls were just freshly invented as part of a year 2000 correction effort. To demonstrate reasonableness, it is necessary to show that the activity under question, in this case the standardization of data element names and codes, was a normal part of organizational technology management and not a one time special event. It is the process that counts, not necessarily the isolated act.

The same need to show control processes as a normal day-to-day activity and not a special event is true for the remaining system management elements as well.

DATABASE MANAGEMENT

Demonstrating sound management of the enterprise's information assets requires more than just the policy of adhering to standard data element names and code representations. Reasonableness would require that industry recognized database management controls be practiced. These practices find their origins in the CODASYL standards and are generally incorporated into commercial database management systems (DBMS). These systems are managed by database administrators (DBA) who must devise an organizational management body to define, review, and enforce data management policies across the enterprise. For reasonableness of DBMS action regarding the year 2000 problem to be believed, the involvement of a database management body and execution of a data control process must be evident through documentation.

DATA ACCESS CONTROLS AND INTEGRITY

Closely related to database management issues are the security access controls placed on system data stores and software programs necessitated by the need to protect proprietary, sensitive, classified, and personal data. These requirements, some of which are legal responsibilities, result in the placing of access and limited use controls on data stores and software programs, depending upon the stringency of the need for security and the job duties of persons accessing the data or seeking to execute some software program.

There is a very real possibility that, in the confusion associated with bringing software and systems into year 2000 compliance, security will be compromised and that breaches of confidentiality will occur and fraudulent action initiated. During remediation and testing, software and systems will be especially vulnerable to tampering. Reasonableness, as a defense, will require that, based on risk, special security controls be considered and placed on the systems if appropriate. Any risk analysis and subsequent decision regarding special security controls need to be documented and kept for the duration of the remediation effort. Once again, the purpose is to be able to demonstrate that the processing environment, during the period of year 2000 conversion, was under strict management control. Anything less is to admit to a lack of due diligence in protecting the interests of all parties during a period of anticipated upheaval when vulnerabilities were likely to be high.

For more on special security considerations during year 2000 remediation efforts, see Appendix B, Year 2000 Date Conversion Management Considerations.

COMPUTING ASSET MANAGEMENT DOCUMENTATION

Although mentioned in previous sections, this documentation deserves to be addressed in greater detail here.

Computing asset management deals with the acquisition, use, control, and disposition of the hardware, software, communications, and personnel resources required to create and operate a computing capability. In other than single vendor environments, complexity can quickly become so great as to require formal and documented computing asset management processes and procedures. The purpose of such processes is to apply the same degree of management discipline that is exercised over other enterprise assets to the domain of information technology and its uses. Historically, large system investments in mainframes and software development were subject to procurement rules and cost/benefit studies while computer utilization was closely monitored in order to reconcile vendor billings and maintenance charges. Software had its own evolving methodologies, and structured techniques came to be applied to the development process in order to improve the likelihood of delivering software that satisfied a user's need at a reasonable cost. It is possible in a mature centralized mainframe environment to demonstrate the same good asset management practices that are used in other departments of the company.

The situation is generally bleaker where decentralized distributed computer processing constitutes the predominate enterprise model. The evolution of distributed computing capabilities is largely to blame for the absence of controls and management. Distributed computing systems have tended to grow from the small to the large—stand alone PCs, to the sharing of common resources (i.e., printers), to networked PCs, to shared mid-size computer resources (i.e., software utilities and access routes to larger systems and networks), to the worldwide capabilities of the Internet. At some point, distributed computing became very large indeed; but computing asset management has not kept pace, so the ability to effectively control distributed computing environments has been missing.

This lack of asset management control in the distributed computing environment has been recently highlighted by the much publicized realization that more than a few enterprises have, over the last several years, paid many more millions of dollars for personal computers and other computing assets than was necessary had competition and negotiated volume pricing been used. Instead of employing sound procurement practices common to the centralized mainframe environments, business units have proceeded to "build out" their computing capability in a small purchase, piecemeal fashion that has been very costly.

Problems with computing asset management are important to a year 2000 reasonable care posture because, as stated in previous sections, the ability to demonstrate management control is essential to being able to demonstrate reasonableness of action. If it is unreasonable to pay many more millions of dollars for computing assets than is necessary, and this can be attributed to an absence of commonly accepted asset management practices, then so may the unreasonableness of year 2000 program actions be attributed to the absence of other common asset management practices.

Let us now examine certain commonly accepted computing asset management practices, and the documentation by-products of each, that may be called into evidence should year 2000 program actions prove less then effective.

SYSTEMS DEVELOPMENT PROCESS

Over the last several decades, improvements have been made in the way software and systems are developed. These improvements are generally of a process nature and impose a discipline based on the thought process associated with problem solving. At the core of many similar methodologies is the systems development process (SDP) comprised of the following sequential steps:

- Requirement definition.
- Analysis and design.
- Development.
- Testing.
- User acceptance.
- Production.

Each of these steps builds on the work accomplished in the previous step. The work products of a step constitute the method of communicating the results of the analytic thought process of that step to the next sequential step in the process, which must have instructions from the previous step in order to continue the progression. Any failure to accomplish a step or to document the thought process of the step compromises the likelihood of meeting the requirement and satisfying the original intent of the system. What is important from a year 2000 problem perspective is that such documentation will prove absolutely essential to making effective fixes and conducting tests of the systems.

Although the logic of following a disciplined and progressive methodology during systems development is hard to refute, the information technology industry has, on the whole, a poor record when it comes to adherence. For reasons we won't explore here,* most systems development efforts cut analytic corners, cheated on adequate testing, and failed to do a complete job of the one activity of development that holds the whole thing together—documentation. The same documentation that is now needed to show that software and systems were under such stringent management control that your year 2000 actions will be accepted as well thought out and reasonable. Again, if it can't be shown that software and systems were comprehensible and under management control, how can any year 2000 action be judged adequate within the requirement to demonstrate reasonable care? Of course, you may claim that the enterprise did the best it could under unmanageable circumstances, but what will that admission do for stock prices and business orders, not to mention careers?

Beyond software and systems for which the enterprise bears developmental responsibility, looms the myriad of hardware and software systems, packages, networks, and wide area communications upon which the enterprise depends for day-to-day business operations. Is it possible that these supporting system developers and integrators also cut analytic corners, cheated on testing, and failed to generate documentation adequate to effect year 2000 fixes and future sustainable operations? In Chapter 5, vendor support agreements and contracts will be addressed; but agreements and contracts, even those with liquidated damages clauses, offer small comfort when the enterprise is unable to operate, revenues are disappearing, and customers are shopping elsewhere.

---

*See Suggested References.

CONFIGURATION MANAGEMENT
AND CHANGE CONTROLS

Assuming that software and system's SDP documentation problems don't exist or can be overcome through a retroactive documentation initiative, there remains the issues of configuration management (CM) and change control. Change control is an activity that falls within the larger challenge of controlling the configurations of hardware and software that make up the operational production systems. These activities maintain the operational integrity of well-tested software and systems during and after the developmental process. CM and change control are themselves processes that prevent the garden of a well-managed development effort from reverting to weeds. As processes, CM and change control adhere to a specific sequence of actions that allow changes, both hardware and software, into operation production environments; but only after the potential impact is analyzed and each change is tested to preclude adverse impacts on a heretofore reliable operating environment.

CM and change control, to be effective, must begin with the documentation that describes the component baseline (i.e., as is) system and maintains this baseline to reflect all subsequent allowable changes. To be effective, CM and change control must be stringently enforced. These two management control activities need to be viewed as the last line of defense standing between a dependable operational production environment and the insertion of faulty code or equipment that can corrupt the environment and destroy the ability to continue processing.

CM and change control are important during the year 2000 corrective actions program because once software and systems are fixed and tested to demonstrate year 2000 compliance, they run the risk of being recontaminated by other ongoing system modifications. Unless comprehensive CM and change control processes are in place, it is not reasonable to assume that all that could be done was done to prevent a recontamination of remediated systems. The ability to demonstrate that CM and change control procedures were in place and properly operating will be necessary to support a claim of reasonable care as part of a defense strategy.

TEST MANAGEMENT AND DOCUMENTATION

In the discussion on the system development process (SDP), it was pointed out that the majority of information technology organizations have, in the course of a software or systems project, cut corners with regard to testing and documentation. Justifications offered include the mathematically true argument that comprehensive testing of all possible software logic paths and processing conditions in even a modest program is theoretically impossible. This argument can be presented with such a tone of resignation as to impart an underlying message that since mathematical certitude is impossible, why bother. Another favorite argument for justifying limited testing during the SDP is that software goes through a series of preproduction releases to knowledgeable customers who essentially assist with testing. These BETA releases are used throughout the commercial industry and within organizations with internally developed software. BETA testers attempt to use the software and report the problems they encounter to the developers. Finally, the most common justification for insufficient testing is the straightforward statement that "the release schedule did not allow enough time."

For all of these reasons, it is not uncommon to find that software and systems testing is an ad hoc affair, carried out by programmers based on their personal career experience with testing. To the extent that formal testing occurs, it is a relatively new affair brought about by recent quality assurance improvement initiatives. For this reason, comprehensive test material (i.e., plans, cases, data, and criteria) won't exist for most older software, while systems integrations testing is generally a case-by-case undertaking with few reproducible test materials.

Testing of year 2000 remediations pose special problems for those asked to gather reasonable care documentation. Since original test materials may not exist for software and systems under remediation, there is little upon which to build year 2000 tests. While straight-forward date value advancement tests (i.e., checking the freshly remediated software and file data for proper processing with a post-2000 date) can determine the validity of a change at the individual program level, it requires a much more complete set of system test materials to confidently affirm that the entire business application is functioning properly in all its operations and in all its exchanges of information with other systems. A complete set of test materials would include those that allow tests to be conducted in the following areas.

- *Program testing:* Coded units are tested for design integrity, conformance, and operability as a program.
- *Integration testing:* Individual programs that have been unit tested after remediation changes are integrated with other programs into applications and tested again for stability and interoperability.

- *Regression testing:* Applications are subjected to their entire suite of tests, not just year 2000 tests, to insure that during the process of remediation nothing else in the program was made inoperable.
- *System testing:* Real world production scenarios are run to insure that system functionality is intact.
- *Interoperability testing:* Assures that year 2000 corrections of different systems will still operate together.
- *Performance testing:* Ensure that system processing resources are sufficient, after remediation, to meet the service level expectations of the user.
- *Stress testing:* Verifies that a remediated system can withstand multiple users under a variety of operating conditions.
- *Destructive testing:* Confirms error detection routines, system recovery procedures and security controls are still operational.
- *Bridge testing:* Checks all date translation routines between compliant and non-compliant programs and systems.
- *User acceptance testing:* End-to-end production testing, often in parallel with the live system, to insure proper processing of the entire business application.
- *Documentation verification:* Manuals and other documents are reviewed for consistency, technical accuracy, and adherence to post-year 2000 processing procedures.

The most critical, but least likely to be possible, is regression testing where all previous tests are rerun, after a software change, to ensure that the change didn't trigger defects or failures elsewhere in the code. Each of the other tests are conducted to confirm that operational compatibilities, performance level, and special features, such as security controls, are all operating within tolerances. In other words, the system is ready for production workloads.

Without these tests, it is going to be difficult to claim that reasonable testing occurred within any definition of industry best practices. Coupled with this difficulty is the fact that few enterprises know how to conduct comprehensive testing. Testing has always been considered a poor career path for information technology professionals; not nearly as glamorous and challenging as the creativeness of development and certainly not as lucrative as project management or sales and marketing. As was pointed out in Chapter 1, testing isn't even deemed to be worthy of inclusion in most university curriculum.

Of the few sources of experienced testers, one seems to be software product companies who are committed to quality or must comply with regulations such as the FDA's G.M.P. for software. Another source is contractors who specialize in doing independent validation verification and testing of software and systems being developed for the government or large corporations. Beyond these two sources are the private consultants who have concentrated their careers in the area of software quality assurance.

To be sure, year 2000 test management and the ability to produce sufficient documentary evidence that reasonable testing took place, poses a serious challenge to most organizations. But, according to most year 2000 project plans, comprehensive testing, across the enterprise, will probably not begin until 1999. If the enterprise understands what is at stake and if professional test expertise can be acquired, then management should use the remaining months of 1998 assembling test materials and developing plans for final systems and user acceptance testing to be conducted in 1999. What cannot be allowed to happen is for the ingrained cultural reluctance to realistically deal with testing to continue. Enough time remains to make a good faith effort to conduct effective year 2000 testing. Failure to demonstrate substantial efforts during this period will undoubtedly be used as a counterargument to those who claim they took a reasonable approach to testing, but that the problems were simply too great.

So far, the topics covered in this chapter have dealt with those traditional elements of information technology management associated with core business systems. These are the management control topics in which any seasoned computer professional should be well versed. We will now address the less traditional area of personal computer (PC) management and identify those elements of documentary evidence that may be required to show that the year 2000 problem was reasonably addressed and under control.

PCs: SPECIAL YEAR 2000 CONCERNS

Many have implied that the year 2000 problem doesn't have much impact on personal computers. However, like every other aspect of this problem, the more an assumption is examined the more troublesome it becomes. A few facts to put the importance of the PC problem into perspective:

- Many PCs use two-digit year representations in both hardware and software systems. As recently as winter 1997, brand new pentiums have failed compliance tests.

- More than 80 million PCs are known to have non-compliant Basic Input Output System (BIOS) chips and hundreds of commercial off-the-shelf software packages with year 2000-related problems are installed on those millions of systems.

- Many millions of small and mid-size businesses do accounting and other date data-related business functions on PCs running Windows 3.1 and older software such as forecasting, human resources, interest calculations, marketing/customer tracking, postage systems, imaging and document processing, local area networks, e-mail, electronic commerce, spreadsheets, inventory control, word processing, workflow control, process control, database management, project planning, electronic preparation of payroll and tax reporting, and automated systems backups.

- As the applications listed above indicate, the size of a business doesn't lessen the complexity of managing it, the degree of computer dependence, or the adverse impact to be experienced when systems fail to operate properly.

- While the individual small business loss* may seem insignificant when compared to the loss experienced by a Fortune 500 company, the cumulative economic effect may well exceed Fortune 500 losses. And since small business reportedly employs 8 of every 10 workers, the impact on public assistance and unemployment benefit systems may be very large indeed. Also, as business revenues drop off, tax collections will be reduced and the ability to continue funding public assistance programs will become a challenging problem for governments committed to deficit or tax reduction.

- Most small and mid-size businesses don't have the cash flows and reserves to upgrade entire suites of PCs and software in the next year, not to mention the added workload of converting files and performing new system insertions into their workplace. Such unplanned expenses and business disruptions will undoubtedly force

---

*During the summer of 1997, various sources estimated that close to 50 percent of American businesses would not be year 2000 compliant in time. (How this translates into lost revenue can only be surmised.)

some borderline operations over the line and into bankruptcy. It may not even be a difficult choice for some owners to make.

Essentially, the activities required to effectively manage a PC-based year 2000 problem are the same as with the largest computer environment at a Fortune 500 company. A complete inventory of PC hardware, peripherals, software and user-developed software, databases, and spreadsheets must be developed and validated. While many package software vendors will upgrade their products to be year 2000 compliant, it is the homegrown software and vendor modified package that will cause serious problems and must be accounted for early in the remediation process. For PC-based business systems, where the enterprise doesn't own the source code or software they are using, it becomes essential to show that the company made an effort to contact each vendor to determine when replacement hardware and upgraded software were to be made available and what vendor-provided conversion software or consultant services are available to assist with the migration to the new system.

Fortune 500 companies as well as any large enterprise have a distinct advantage in obtaining the support necessary to fix their year 2000 problem They are big—they do business with big information technology providers and their fates are mutually bound together. Together, they usually work something out to protect the interests of both parties. The admonition of caveat emptor—let the buyer beware—takes on meaning when a small company deals with a small information technology provider. Neither small business can withstand the disruption in cash flow brought about by failed systems. The small business can't muster the resources to sue and the small provider can't pay if held liable. Nobody wins and everyone loses. The principal protection for the small business is to require, and pay for, extensive testing to prove the readiness of all system upgrades and modifications. The small company cannot afford the luxury of back-up processes and procedures should the computer system fail to operate properly. The small company can't afford to hire temporary help to answer phones and do business manually. If anything, the small company, dependant on PC-based processing, must be more confident of year 2000 readiness than the large Fortune 500 counterpart.

From a reasonable care perspective, documentation requirements consist primarily of inventories and asset management information describing the configuration. Other elements of documentation deal with hardware and software vendors, and your information technology outsourcer, if appropriate. These types of documents will be discussed in the next chapter.

ESSENTIAL SYSTEMS DOCUMENTATION

This chapter identified those elements of hardware, software, and network management documentation that may be needed to demonstrate that systems supporting the enterprise are under control and that reasoned, deliberate year 2000 plans and actions can be assessed to have emanated from such an environment. Year 2000 fixes are required everywhere in the information technology environment and will touch all computing assets. It is not reasonable to claim that actions taken to correct problems in an uncontrolled environment could be as effective as actions taken in a well-managed environment. This is at the heart of the reasonable care defense, which is really an exercise in risk management. In an imperfect world, it is possible to be wrong, but reasonable in action as long as consistent effort was made to know and understand the risk. But it is not possible to claim reasonableness of action if the risk wasn't even knowable, due to uncontrolled conditions in the operating environment or a lack of documentation. If a correct action was taken within an uncontrolled and unmanageable operating environment, it could be considered lucky but hardly reasoned.

5

YEAR 2000 PROJECT DOCUMENTATION

Each previous chapter has identified documentation that indicates that an enterprise has been controlling its information technology assets according to sound management principles and practices. By being able to demonstrate management control, it is far more likely that an enterprise will be able to claim that it addressed, with reasonable care, the year 2000 problem. Documentary evidence will show that the enterprise was capable and diligent, because of its comprehensive knowledge of the processing systems and customer uses of its date-related data. Evidence also needs to show that the enterprise conducted risk assessments, identified all data stores and processing software, located all hardware systems and network elements, made and tested corrections, and communicated to all affected parties information concerning progress and unresolved risks. Without such documentation, it may well prove difficult to convince an objective observer that a reasonable approach was followed in solving the year 2000 problem.

This chapter will identify and discuss those elements of documentation that will be needed to convince an objective observer that the year 2000 project was, itself, carried out in a manner that followed sound project management principles and could therefore be considered a reasonable effort at problem solving and risk containment.

TOP MANAGEMENT SUPPORT AND THE PROJECT MANAGEMENT OFFICE

Was there ever an undertaking that didn't claim to need top management support in order to succeed? This is especially true of a year 2000 project for several reasons, including:

- Documentary evidence of top management pronouncements concerning the seriousness of the year 2000 problem are needed to meet some of the requirements of Chapter 2, but more importantly, they are needed to provide a focus for the enterprise. Somehow, the projected importance of these pronouncements needs to raise the year 2000 issue above the normal degree of seriousness imparted by the typical executive utterances supporting the most recent management fad. A series of quarterly reports "to all concerned," showing progress and problem areas, would satisfy this need. By focusing attention over many months, the seriousness of the issue begins to be evident and continuous communications with employees, customers, and other interested parties, from the highest organizational levels, can be shown to have occurred.

- Mid-level managers and employees accomplish what they perceive to be important and that for which they are held accountable. If the accomplishment of year 2000 corrective actions is perceived to be just another work task competing with all other tasks, managers and employees will attempt to accomplish all tasks with no special emphasis given to any particular one. Priorities are important and generally are established by executive management. If the "computer catastrophe of the century" is treated as just another ho-hum priority one task (after all, everything is priority one in many organizations), it will take on no greater urgency than installing a new database package for yet another pilot project.

Top management needs to empower the year 2000 effort with an executive level charter supported by the proponents of all potentially competing projects. In the charter, roles and responsibilities are identified and the commitment needed to meet the goals and objectives of the charter are agreed to by all executives whose support is required.

A program management office (PMO) needs to be established and staffed with permanent personnel and a budget. The PMO must be authorized to form directing committees to oversee planning and execution of remedial actions throughout the enterprise. Persons appointed to year 2000 committees should be senior enough to speak for their organizational element, and for the sake of continuity, must be expected to stay on the committee for the duration. Meetings, deliberations, recommendations, and decisions should be documented in meeting minutes.

It should be clear from the documentary evidence that the PMO had senior executive and board of director access, and that periodic status reports were rendered to these groups for their information and action. If decentralized implementation of year 2000 corrective actions is expected, then status reports to the PMO, from the implementing units, need to be a matter of record.

COMPREHENSIVE INVENTORIES DEMONSTRATE CONTROL

Chapter 4 addressed this requirement at length; inventories need to be included as a specific element of the year 2000 documentation package. Inventory documentation provides the baseline knowledge to support all subsequent decisions, plans, and actions to be taken during the remediation effort. The process to be used for maintaining inventory accuracy and currency should be documented and available for review. For most elements of the systems inventory, the configuration management and change control system discussed in Chapter 4 should suffice. It is desirable to show that the impact assessment and management review steps of the CM procedures were not by-passed in emergency fix situations. But if they were, it is imperative to show that retroactive reviews were carried out as soon after the emergency fix as possible. All changes to hardware, software, datebase, or communication networks must be accounted for from a year 2000 perspective or else the completeness of year 2000 remediation actions will be in doubt.

RISK ASSESSMENT AND TRIAGE DECISIONS

As the year 2000 countdown continues, it becomes likely that triage decisions, concerning which systems to fix or replace first and which to delay for correction, will be challenged by organizational elements who weren't paying close attention when such decisions were initially made. Suddenly, it will occur to some vice president that a system in his area of responsibility has been put on the noncritical mission list and deferred for corrective action. This realization will spark an intense interest in how earlier triage decisions were made and how it was that his "noncritical system" made it to the deferred list. The PMO needs to be prepared with documentary evidence as to how the original risk assessment was conducted and how triage decisions were made and who approved each decision.

The same issue of how triage decisions were made is also likely to be raised in any challenge to show reasonable care. Any business partner or customer group harmed by a year 2000 system failure, especially if the system was deferred for correction, will challenge the triage decision. The enterprise may be required to justify, not necessarily the decision, but the process by which the decision was made. To do this, each decision to fix or defer a system must be tied to the critical nature of a business function or to the determined potential for damage to a business partner, customer, or innocent third party. All such relationships and decisions must be documented and retained by the PMO.

As time passes from the date of an original triage decision, events may occur that could affect the initial determination. It would be advisable to periodically revisit all earlier triage decisions for continued validity as the year 2000 remediation program progresses. It is highly possible that many early corrective strategies, based on anticipated fixes coming from other technology providers or system replacement projects, cannot be implemented. Dependent as they were on external compliance actions of others, they will not be implemented in time if any of these actions falter.

CONTINGENCY PLANNING

Each triage decision and its accompanying corrective action strategy and project plan needs to have a contingency plan that is re-examined periodically for continuing reasonableness. In fact, several contingency plans or fall back options may be needed depending upon when it becomes clear that the original goal of system compliance is not going to be realized. At the heart of each of these contingency plans or fall back options is the requirement to keep all impacted and interested parties thoroughly informed of the conditions that have triggered the need to invoke the back-up plan and an honest appraisal of whether or not the contingent actions will meet the deadline for compliance. If changes to business as usual, such as the hiring of temporary employees to assist with manual processing, are anticipated, each impacted party must be informed of this in time to make appropriate procedural adjustments. Failure to do so, leaving business partners and customers in the dark until the normal business process fails, will undoubtedly result in litigation. Such failures to communicate would hardly convince an objective observer that the secretive enterprise was concerned about their business partners or customers, and certainly would not demonstrate reasonable care.

PROJECT PLANS FOR YEAR 2000 REMEDIATIONS

It may seem that the previous section on contingency plans should come after this discussion of year 2000 project plans. The reason for the reversal is deliberate, however, and is related to the fact that contingency planning is usually an afterthought in most information technology planning efforts since it is generally thought of after a failure has occurred. In the case of year 2000 remediation project plans, the safe and reasonable course for planning is to assume failure and think in terms of contingency plans. This way, the tendency toward overly optimistic estimates and schedules, which is a habit of information technology planners, will be tempered from the outset by survival thinking.

Year 2000 remediation project planning must consciously proceed at three levels:

1. There must be overall enterprise level compliance planning to assure that all aspects of the business or agency operations necessary for continued viability are included.
2. Specific business system compliance planning should occur with the technology portion of the system being kept in its appropriately subordinate role. This positioning of technology support systems within the larger business activity keeps the year 2000 problem properly focused as a business problem and not just a technical challenge to be solved by computer people while the rest of the enterprise goes about their business.
3. Year 2000 remediation efforts should plan on not being completely implemented in the little time remaining and contingency plans should focus on "nonelectronic" alternatives.

Project managers should expect to have their plans scrutinized and evaluated as to their reasonableness and as to the comprehensive thoroughness they exhibit. A major aspect of this reasonableness criteria will be whether or not each individual plan, and the overall enterprise plan as well, planned for failure. Were there contingent actions central to their focus?

The plans themselves need to contain all the standard ingredients required to direct and monitor the accomplishment of any complex undertaking.* There must be clear and concise statements of expectations and objectives. Assumptions and constraints, especially external dependencies, need to be stated up front. Statements of work need to be generated for precisely defined tasks. Work breakdown structures should be developed for each task with essential resource requirements identified. Resources should include funding, hardware, software, tools, personnel, time estimates, training, and consultant or contract resources.

Schedules and milestones need to be identified for individual tasks, with enterprisewide critical paths determined for the successful integration of tasks across organizational boundaries. Project status and progress review milestones need to be established, which identify at which time risk factors are to be examined and contingent actions developed as required.

Executive presentations need to be conducted on a regular basis with required attendance by those with a fiduciary or other legal responsibility. Independent validation reviews by auditors or external subject area specialists such as testers or security experts need to be reported through a separate chain of command to the PMO or the board of directors.

Periodic reports to business partners, customers, investors, regulatory officials, and potentially impacted third parties need to be communicated in a manner and in a timeframe sufficient to allow appropriate actions to be taken by all affected parties.

Within the context of an overall year 2000 remediation project plan are a series of subordinate technology and management control subplans and activities. The following sections address those plans and activities that have a direct relationship to the technology strategy selected for solving the remediation challenge. Whether the technology strategy is date field expansion, programming logic changes such as windowing, bridge software between systems for translation purposes or the wholesale replacement of noncompliant systems with compliant ones, these plans and activities need to be carried out to insure success and demonstrate that reasonable care was exercised.

---

* See Suggested References for excellent books covering the specifics of project management.

SUPPLIER AGREEMENTS AND
CONTRACT LANGUAGE

One of the first actions to be taken by any enterprise is to prevent a continuation of year 2000 problem conditions into the future. It is difficult to imagine that any vendor would, during the summer and fall of 1998, sell noncompliant hardware, software, or turn-key services to any customer, but not impossible. In the confusion that surrounds this issue, there are no universally accepted definitions of compliance and probably won't be until well after the year 2000 when the courts will be forced to make rulings. Without enforceable definitions, some suppliers will undoubtedly take advantage of the situation and knowingly sell noncompliant products to unsuspecting consumers.

Until the courts do become involved, which will be too late for those whose business or life has been disrupted, organizations must endeavor to deal with the problem in spite of existing standard warranty language and contract clauses that favor the supplier.

There are two courses of action open to the consumer. If the customer is a business entity, special contractual language can be put in place to protect the interests of the company. Companies and government agencies should propose their own contract terms and conditions and negotiate year 2000 compliance language with their suppliers. Penalties, by way of liquidated damages clauses, should be included so as to be clear about the risks involved and to demonstrate the seriousness of the problem in the mind of the buyer. This approach will work only in certain instances where the business has a great deal of leverage. The second course of action is similar to the first in that it reminds the supplier that future business dealings will be put at risk should your enterprise suffer year 2000 damages because of their products, or because of their supplier's products. Remind suppliers that your company is very active in the Chamber of Commerce and knows how the Better Business Bureau works. Certain large corporations, such as those in the automotive industry, have jointly defined year 2000 standards to be adhered to by their suppliers, and have initiated programs to assist suppliers to reach compliance. They have sent a very clear message that none but the very foolish would ignore.

From a reasonable care perspective, it is important to show that steps were taken not only to communicate the year 2000 requirements of your company to suppliers, but also to demonstrate that supplier compliance had been negotiated and was expected, through either specific contract terms or by clear correspondence to the supplier that loss of future business orders will be experienced by those vendors who supply noncompliant products.

It is essential that legal counsel be consulted when dealing with vendor and supplier issues. Equally important is the role of legal advice when negotiating agreements with your customers.

YEAR 2000 COMPLIANCE AND CERTIFICATIONS

Another aspect of vendor and supplier management is to be on record as having inquired about product certifications. Certain industry groups such as the Information Technology Association America (ITAA) have instituted an accreditation program whereby the processes used by a vendor in developing a product or delivering an analytic service are evaluated against the best practices of the industry. If the vendor or supplier satisfies the scrutiny of a third-party evaluator, in this case, the Software Productivity Consortium, ITAA will issue a certification of year 2000 compliance. Such a certification is not a guarantee or warranty, but a studied judgment by knowledgeable professionals that if the processes they observed are, in fact, adhered to, it is probable that a soundly developed product or service will result—and be likely to stand up to year 2000 processing demands.

The processes that are examined to determine soundness of developmental methods are those addressed in Chapter 4. The same asset management and systems development processes and practices will be called into evidence to claim reasonable care should a company be sued for damages due to non-year 2000 compliant date processing.

CUSTOMER COMMUNICATIONS

In the previous section, the importance of vendor and supplier communications was emphasized; here the other side of the coin is addressed, since your enterprise also functions as a vendor and supplier to your customers. What sort of documentary evidence will be needed to convince an objective observer that your customers were kept in your year 2000 problem-solving loop? The ITAA has recommended to its memberships that vendors should provide all the year 2000 information possible, in a cooperative fashion, to their customers. It is the opinion of ITAA's legal staff that such communications will greatly reduce liability suits because of the mitigating nature of the action. It is not clear, however, if such proactive communication will have any affect on stockholder or third-party suits.

Nevertheless, open communications with your customers concerning your year 2000 problem, solutions in progress, and possible adverse impacts would seem to form the basis for demonstrating reasonable care. What form should these communiques take?

If your enterprise develops hardware, software, or turn-key systems, such as medical devices, where the technology is embedded into the product, straightforward announcements regarding current year 2000 compliance of products in use is a necessity. This information should include a clear description of products that are compliant and those that are not. If replacement year 2000 compliant products are to be offered, that should be made clear with a schedule as to when such products will be available to the customer. If upgrades or patches constitute bringing a product into compliance this should be communicated, again with a schedule as to when the fix will be available. In both cases, an estimate of cost to the customer should be conveyed for their planning purposes. If products are bundled with other software and systems from different suppliers, the product provider assumes responsibility for compliance of these systems that they have included in their complete package. This means that interoperable aspects of the total package must be carefully tested and documented.

As the ITAA has advised, communications should be open and proactive. The Internet can be used for this purpose, but not relied on solely. Everyone in a customer contact position should be sensitive to year 2000 inquiries as well and be able to provide information to customers. People will long remember if they feel they are getting the run-around. Copies of all communications should be retained to demonstrate that a reasonable effort was made to keep the consumer and your business partners informed of year 2000 developments.

As of the fall of 1997, there was a decided lack of information from suppliers concerning readiness of their products to handle year 2000 date processing. By summer of 1998, this will undoubtedly improve because customers will be in the final stages of overall year 2000 remediation activities and must have compliant hardware and software from their suppliers to be able to proceed with 1999 system acceptance testing. If suppliers and products are no more forthcoming by then, it will indicate a much larger problem than anyone would like to contemplate.

Suppliers that are following the advice of the ITAA will be able to demonstrate a degree of reasonableness, in the face of adversity, that will be hard to challenge. Those that don't may be open to severe criticism, legal action, and loss of market share.

TEST PLANS AND REASONABLE CARE DEFENSE

It will be absolutely impossible to defend a liability suit with a claim that reasonable care was taken in correcting the year 2000 problem if testing was not a major part of the overall remediation effort. This one area poses a special threat because so few computer-dependent enterprises have ever employed good test practices in their rush to field systems. In Chapter 4, weak testing practices and test documentation were addressed from the perspective of being able to demonstrate management control over the computing assets of the enterprise. Here, the concern centers on countering risks of business failures through the specifics of testing corrected systems and systems which are advertised as being year 2000 compliant. Any organization that cannot point to a robust testing initiative will be easy prey during litigation. Reasonable care dictates that considerable effort be spent in testing. Furthermore, reasonable care would seem to require that customers and business partners, at the least, be alerted to year 2000 product problems, and this can't be accomplished without a testing effort to uncover date processing defects.

Some will argue that no amount of testing is ever adequate, the subliminal message being why bother, everyone knows software has "bugs." This is true, but not sufficient to argue against reasonable care. Reason dictates that, in an imperfect world, testing take place to a degree commensurate with the risk to be incurred should the software fail. Thus, in situations where life and limb could be at risk should software fail, much more extensive testing would be reasonable than in a situation where mere convenience is at risk—such as an automated teller machine failure. The extent of testing is therefore directly related to anticipated risks or loss to be experienced should software or system failure occur. The comprehensiveness of testing is therefore linked to both Chapter 2 risk assessments and to triage decisions which selected the mission-critical systems and software to be first remediated.

The importance of a risk-driven testing strategy cannot be over emphasized. In October 1997, news reports were just surfacing that a software "glitch," a euphemism for failure, in at least one and possibly two systems contributed to the fatal crash of Korean Air Flight 801. The minimum safe altitude warning system failed to report to the air controllers that the plane was too low on the approach to landing, and warnings could not be issued to the pilot. This is a system that is used at 214 airports nationwide. A second warning system in the cockpit also seems to have failed to alert the pilot to the fact that the plane was descending too rapidly. This is also a software dependent system. While not date-related, these examples, in addition to being spectacular, represent the increasing dependence on software systems where life and limb may be at stake. The preface listed the categories of business, government, and infrastructure support systems that are heavily automated and upon which society depends greatly. When formulating the test strategy for a year 2000 remediation effort, it is advisable to review that list against your applications and take extra precautions to ensure that the degree and extent of year 2000 testing is commensurate with potential risks.

QUALITY ASSURANCE PLANS AND REVIEWS

The PMO, in addition to accomplishing each of activities listed in this chapter, must ensure the quality of work products if reasonable care is to be claimed. It is advisable to view all year 2000 program activities in the same way as any complex undertaking. It is important that the quality of each analytic step be verified, through a review process, before proceeding with the next step in the activities progression. Collectively, related program activities need to be reviewed for those quality aspects that can effect the total effort. Since year 2000 remediation activities are new to virtually everyone, it is imperative to not cut any quality assurance corners.

Quality assurance generally refers to the process of anticipating defects and flaws in a systems design and development and taking special actions to discover those defects early in the project's life. Quality assurance can be likened to the carpenter's maxim to "measure twice, cut once." Quality assurance techniques insure that this admonition is achieved by concentrating on potential problems inherent to the nature of the system under development. This means that quality assurance should be risk sensitive, requiring additional quality assurance measures on a development effort as risk rises. The more complex and risky an undertaking, the more quality review and validation steps should be imposed on the project.

This approach is in contrast with the generally accepted practices of quality control that tend to concentrate on testing for defects and flaws at the end of a product's development and production phases. In addition to being the most cost inefficient approach to quality, testing only at the conclusion of a year 2000 remediation effort may prove most dangerous. Given the time constraints of the year 2000 deadline, there will most likely be no time remaining to correct defects, if testing is deferred until late in the process. A proactive quality assurance effort, discovering defects, flaws, and other problems early during remediation is a more reasonable way to proceed and much more defensible. Most information technology organizations have some group or a few individuals who over the years have championed quality, usually without too much support from anyone else. Now is the time to draft these people and their expertise in a cause worthy of their previously demonstrated commitment to the organization. They have the knowledge and tools to monitor the remediation effort and provide assessments to the PMO regarding the quality of corrective work being performed. Since, in the interest of time, testing should be conducted on an "as you go basis," (see Appendix B) quality assurance practices should facilitate the efforts between remediation personnel and testers. Concurrent engineering concepts being applied to the remediation/test process can, if implemented along with quality assurance techniques, deliver year 2000 corrected systems in a much shorter time than traditional methods.

INDEPENDENT VALIDATION AND VERIFICATION

By the summer and fall of 1998, organizations should be completing remediation actions on systems and software that are critical. It is time to consider the independent validation and verification (IVV) of systems as an insurance policy against surprises in 1999, when parallel processing and user acceptance is scheduled to occur. Independent tests of remediated systems can be conducted by personnel in the enterprise separate from those involved in remediation and its limited testing. Alternatively, outside contractor testing can be arranged. Independent testing should begin by attempting to execute, on a random or sample basis, the same tests used by the remediation group. It would be advisable to conduct such tests on high-risk applications and on the year 2000 compliant mainframe and local area network configurations. Applications that perform date data calculations and all financial management, inventory, personnel, and benefit disbursement systems should be high on the list for an independent appraisal. Equally important would be order

entry systems and those that have a direct impact on any business partner. Of special concern are systems such as medical devices, air traffic
control, and other process control systems, where property and life and
limb are potentially at risk.

Independent appraisals of the readiness of a system for year 2000 processing should be a key element in a strategy to show reasonable care. To
depend solely on the testing provided by the remediation group, with their
programmer's limited experience in testing, is to invite criticism should
the system fail and it can be shown that time was available for a more
comprehensive approach. Independent validation and verification should
be conducted in accordance with the quality assurance model of progressive reviews throughout the life of the remediation effort. IVV can
also be employed to review the effectiveness of any system work-arounds
that need to be devised and used until delayed system elements can be
deemed year 2000 compliant. A major area in the work-around category
is the use of bridge software between systems to translate noncompliant
date data into something usable by the receiving application. Bridges will
likely see extensive service during the early months of year 2000 when
many systems, which need to be compatible, are in various stages of final
testing and are not yet ready to directly communicate date data with each
other. Since bridge software will be so critical to meeting continued business requirements, each should be tested exhaustively under a variety of
operational conditions.

IVV should also be considered as a final check for any firewall software that may be installed for the expressed purpose of protecting the
compliant data stores of the enterprise from outside contamination. Fire-
walls establish access controls over any process attempting to communicate with highly critical business processing systems that have been made
year 2000 compliant. They provide state-of-the-art protection against
accidental or deliberate insertions of noncompliant date data into the
processing environment of the enterprise and should be thoroughly tested
to determine dependability. A decision to use some amount of IVV is
encouraged because it makes good sense and because it provides com-
pelling evidence that reasonable care was exercised.

END-USER PC REMEDIATION ASSISTANCE

As mentioned in Chapter 4, there are at least 80 million personal computers in the world with year 2000 problems. The vast majority of these

will require some degree of remediation work. This work will correct or modify basic input output system (BIOS) chips and a great deal of software. PC and software vendors of course would prefer to sell complete upgrades that are compliant as replacement systems, but this solution could prove extremely expensive, especially for small PC-dependent businesses. It could also prove to be a sizeable manufacturing and logistics challenge to replace or upgrade 80 million systems in two years.

Other approaches must be considered by the PMO such as the wholesale re-examination and redefinition of PC usage within the enterprise. The goal of such a re-examination would be to retire and possibly eliminate many PC and software programs from the corporate or agency inventory, concentrating on those applications that truly impact business operations and accelerating their correction. A difficulty arises in identifying all the systems and software that may have infiltrated the enterprise over the past few years. Tools exist that can perform inventory duties running on LAN servers. Such tools automatically collect all hardware and software inventory data within the network. Some inventory tools have been specifically modified to focus on the year 2000-related aspects of the PC network. Once collected, such data can be compared against proprietary databases of year 2000 compliance information being maintained and updated as a service by the tool provider. The value added here is not so much the tool, but the database of compliance information on PC hardware and package software. Some tools can even report on the contents of PC-based spreadsheets and databases to identify date data that will need to be migrated to upgraded or replacement vendor software.

This process of obtaining an inventory and identifying all PC hardware and software facilitates the making of decisions concerning which PC assets actually contribute to the business and which do not. Such information can then be used to determine how much to spend on PC remediation efforts. As was pointed out in a previous chapter, it has recently come to management's attention that the cost of PC ownership often appears to be exceedingly high when compared to value gained. A possible residual benefit of an aggressive year 2000 PC use evaluation initiative might be a substantial reduction in PC inventories and lowered cost of ownership. From the year 2000 perspective, anything the enterprise can do to reduce the size of the problem also reduces risk, costs, and improves the probability of remediation success.

Once essential PC systems and software have been identified for remediation, plans will have to be formulated. The complexity of these implementation plans will be compounded by the need to upgrade or re-place PC-COTS software packages, change existing files to be year 2000 compliant, and retrain end users. All this may prove even more resource intensive than mainframe and legacy system fixes, and justifies a strat-egy of eliminating everything possible from the inventory.

As with mainframe and network assets, it is important to assess and track your PC and software warranties and vendor upgrade policies. In some cases, software has undergone a name change or the licensor has changed names or been subject to a merger or acquisition. Some vendors, especially in the margin slim arena of PC hardware and software, may abandon their products rather than incur the expense of creating compli-ant systems. Some vendors will undoubtedly decide to force an upgrade on the consumer.

End users will need assistance with all these issues and the PMO must be able to provide such help, for it demonstrates that reasonable care was exercised at all levels of the enterprises. To be sure, providing assistance to a widely dispersed PC empire will be formidable, but an effort must be made. Training and consultant services need to be made available to any business unit expressing a requirement. Developing a *PC User's Guide for Year 2000 Compliance* would accomplish a great deal in demonstrat-ing that reasonable care was taken in addressing a most misunderstood aspect of the total year 2000 challenge.

YEAR 2000 PROJECT DOCUMENTATION

This chapter identified the many activities that need to be undertaken and documented regarding the enterprise's year 2000 project manage-ment effort. All reasonable care actions find their justification in the original year 2000 risk analysis that measures the adverse impact of a system failure and determines the priorities in which remediation ac-tions will be taken. All other year 2000 corrective and situation man-agement activities also flow from the risk analysis and from industry best practices.

6

OPERATIONAL CONSIDERATIONS

By the summer and fall of 1998, most organizations will be in the midst of software and systems corrections and testing and will find the pieces more difficult to reassemble than they were to disassemble. Year 2000 remediation teams are likely to experience the fate of the automobile mechanic when faced with the repair of an old engine—pieces are missing, replacement parts can't be found, the schematics don't appear complete and the sludge, formerly engine oil, is providing the principal source of compression. It will never run as before and performance will always be less. With the majority of year 2000 projects the same is going to occur. After remediation, system performance will degrade as a result of additional processing overhead associated with date data bridge software being executed between applications, new program logic that accepts noncompliant dates and makes them useable, and special routines devised to work around code that can't or shouldn't be changed. Each of these examples of additional year 2000-related computer processing needs to be carefully estimated and simulated with anticipated workload volumes to show total system throughput degradation. Response times to customers could suffer appreciably and therefore need to be offset by acquiring greater computing capacity and processor speed so service levels can remain constant.

PERFORMANCE AND CAPACITY PLANNING

With many computer applications, speed of processing is the added value with faster service being the product. If customers suffer lost revenues, even though date data transfers are correct, they may still be tempted to sue for damages, and these damages would be related to the year 2000 problem.

To prevent such legal action, it is advisable to keep service level agreements in mind and monitor the system for postremediation degradations in performance. This must be accomplished throughout year 2000 systems testing, with any slight reduction in performance being recorded and used to project total system degradation under full workloads. It has been estimated that upwards of 20 percent of total year 2000 costs will be for capacity and processor upgrades to compensate for remediation-related losses in through put and response times. This is a sizeable dollar amount to surprise executives with, but is unavoidable if speed and throughput are important.

Capacity management, as an information technology discipline has not entered the year 2000 scene until now, but adverse impacts from the year 2000 problem demand that it be addressed as part of a total remediation program. If capacity shortfall estimates are accurate, there could well be a rush for upgraded equipment that could overwhelm the manufacturers and systems integration providers. Requirements for year 2000-related capacity and processor upgrades should be determined as early in the testing cycle as possible so that enough time is allowed to execute the necessary procurements.

Failure to be able to demonstrate that capacity and processor requirements were being monitored and, if necessary, that upgrade actions were taken, would constitute a failure to show that reasonable care was exercised to prevent adverse impacts on customers, business partners, and others.

YEAR 2000 PERSONNEL RETENTION

An area of great concern to those attempting to solve their year 2000 problem is personnel retention. Whether in-house staff or contractor support, retention of personnel for the duration of a remediation effort is a challenge that will sorely test the best human resources department. The size of the problem, the scarcity of qualified programmers and testers, and the mounting sense of urgency has created an employee's marketplace where competitive rates are increasing monthly. Any enterprise attempting to hire their own year 2000 remediation team or utilizing contractor support must be concerned with high staff turnover rates when no turnover can be tolerated.

There are two aspects to this problem that can only be addressed by senior enterprise executives. First is the issue of guaranteeing, in the case of contractor support, an hourly rate escalation mechanism whereby the contractor can easily pass on to the enterprise the increased costs of retaining remediation team members. Fixed price thinking is not going to get this job done for many reasons, bidding wars for competent and experienced people being one of them. Time and materials contracts are probably the best vehicles. Government agencies have a more difficult time with this problem since they tend to negotiate long-term hourly rates that tend to be difficult to change under prevailing procurement rules. Creative contracting will be needed for the duration of the year 2000 remediation and test period.

The second aspect of the personnel retention challenge deals with employee relations and the structuring of incentive programs. Employment contracts and signing bonuses are useful in this arena. Some organizations have experimented with bonuses based on completing the remediation early but this needs to be carefully considered. First, consider what constitutes completion. Also, consider if one remediation aspect of the total effort is being motivated to speed up its process at the expense of another, namely, code conversion or file expansion activities at the expense of testing and certification. Such incentive ideas need to be carefully reviewed based upon the overall strategy being employed for the project and tailored for maximum retention and productivity, but never at the expense of quality.

One final personnel issue deals not with retention but with trustworthiness. Are the people delving deep into your enterprises' critical systems of high integrity and can they be trusted with sensitive, confidential, and proprietary information? Are they bonded? Have they been subjected to background investigations? Do they possess government clearances? During the chaos of the final months leading up to the millennium roll over, many systems and businesses will be extremely vulnerable to industrial espionage, fraudulent undertakings, and sabotage. No doubt integrity checks on personnel will increase overall cost, but it may be a small price to pay for the peace of mind it brings.

BACK-UP PLANS, DISASTER RECOVERY, AND THE YEAR 2000

A final aspect of information processing and its management that needs to be addressed from a year 2000 perspective is the area of business back-up and disaster recovery plans. In Chapter 5, it was suggested that businesses need to plan to fail. This approach forces the enterprise to focus on contingent actions to keep the vital functions of the business operating should year 2000 remediation efforts fall short. It also takes into account the effect of your year 2000 failure on business partners and customers. The awareness led to the creation of plans to lessen such impacts, and resulted in a documentary trail evidencing that responsible and reasonable care were high on the priority list of executive management.

An essential piece of this strategy would be to insure that all existing business back-up plans are modified to reflect each and every year 2000 remediation action taken to date. This would require the updating of business back-up plans to reflect the year 2000 reality of systems having been remediated according to the triage priorities and schedules. This new collection of compliant applications to be executed at the enterprise's back-up facility will be different than the preyear 2000 remediated systems, and will have to be periodically updated, and tested, as additional remediated applications clear certification testing and are allowed back into the portfolio of systems. In other words, the back-up plans of the enterprise should be included in final year 2000 testing to insure the ability to support the organization in case of an emergency.

Disaster recovery plans pose a different set of problems, especially if they need to be invoked anytime during the period of remediation. This is a problem solved through the discipline of configuration management and change control. As discussed earlier, CM is essential for synchronizing and maintaining the various baselines of system components and software units undergoing remediation, and for insuring that a fall-back configuration is always available for operational emergencies. For disaster recovery, complete mirror images of each computing asset needed to continue operations must be kept at the ready. This will include hardware platforms, located at a geographic distance, software and files, operating instructions, the physical means of transportation, and personnel designated to do the processing. Duplicates of all corrected systems must be retained and maintained equal to their production system counterparts. This will require that frequent updates of back-up software units and system files stay current with those exiting the remediation and test process. The importance of these activities cannot be overemphasized, as many potential failures are possible during the final phase of year 2000 remediation. Despite the best efforts spent on risk assessments and proactive planning, all risks cannot be predicted and unforeseen emergencies will arise.

EMBEDDED MICROCHIP ASSESSMENT PROGRAM

As of this writing, the possibilities for year 2000 problems surrounding the use of microchips seem to be veiled in uncertainty. At potential risk are any systems built around embedded microprocessors. In manufacturing, for example, a process control system may have been developed and programmed on a physical microchip that does not support the date rollover to the year 2000. Microprocessor control systems are everywhere and affect all aspects of contemporary life. They are embedded into everything from medical devices to trucks, trains, and aircraft. There may be over 100 microprocessors in your automobile and they can be found in your new camera. Some systems, such as elevators, have their maintenance periods recorded and tracked by microprocessors that will prevent the system's use if maintenance is overdue. It is a safety feature that could disable many systems, such as the elevator, if the microprocessor thinks that maintenance is years overdue.

The problem stems from the fact that at the heart of all microprocessors is a clock—that is recording the passage of time even when the system appears to be turned off. These clocks initiate the boot-up activities of the system when they are turned on. Whether this basic clock function can handle the date turnover is the question. Are these microchips going to continue operating without a problem?

While outside the realm of the traditional information technology group, the microprocessor issue has found a home there. As though they didn't have enough to do, many information technology organizations are now being expected to determine whether the elevators will work on January 1, 2000, and whether the corporate jet is safe to fly. No one can answer these questions until each and every system that utilizes embedded microchip technology is examined. In the interest of being able to demonstrate that reasonable care was exercised, it is suggested that microprocessor issues be redirected, as necessary, to those who have line responsibility for the systems that are dependent on the embedded chips.

7

CONCLUSION

Less than two years remain before the dire predictions of year 2000 computing problems begin to occur in earnest. This book, which has been presented as an audit guide for executive management, can be used in several ways.

First, it can be ignored, as other books addressing the year 2000 problem have been ignored. But claiming ignorance may not bring much solace as businesses fail, governments can't deliver service, and lawyers begin to gather. Ignorance will be hard to claim given the amount of publicity this topic has received by the summer and fall of 1998.

Wishful thinking (i.e., waiting for a magical solution), may be an unconscious decision to avoid certain facts of life and the realities of a situation by conjuring up a favorable reality and living within it. Wishful thinking, and viewing the world through rose-colored glasses, insulates us from the very facts of life by which we become knowledgeable enough to feel uneasy and eventually take action. Wishful thinkers, knowingly or not, believe that by *not* recognizing a problem it has *no* power over them, when the opposite is true. Wishful thinkers may also tend to ignore the contents of this book.

This book can be viewed as the not too-well disguised opinions of a Luddite, and therefore be dismissed as being irrelevant. Luddite—NO! But this writer does advocate the responsible management of a technology that we have allowed to have such great influence over our society, economy, and personal lives. Responsible management of information technology would include such things as making technology use decisions with some attention being given to the limitations of computers as well as their greatly advertised capabilities. If anything is to be learned from the year 2000 problem it should be that computers do exactly what they are programmed to do. They cannot adjust, to even a seemingly simple challenge, a date interpretation, without extensive reprogramming or redesigning.

Responsible technology management should be risk sensitive, with greater care being taken with high-risk system applications than with low-risk uses. Responsible technology management also requires the exercise of discipline over the development of systems. The higher the system risk, the greater the need for disciplined adherence to the "best practices" of quality assurance and testing before systems delivery. Responsible technology management requires accountability for the consequences of deviating from sound system development methods and taking short-cuts in quality assurance.

This book can be accepted in the spirit in which it was written, as an executive guide for assessing year 2000 progress and for determining the existence and status of year 2000 program documentation that may be eventually required as evidence demonstrating that a reasonable approach was taken in attempts to solve the problem. It is believed that readers, taking the pulse of their year 2000 efforts and coming away alarmed, still have sufficient time remaining to take mitigating actions and thereby reduce their potential liability. The principal mitigating actions that are still available during 1999, if things are going poorly, are to test, test, and test again any system that must be placed back into postyear 2000 productivity. The worst scenario an enterprise can experience is to conduct business with a system that adversely affects others.

The second most critical mitigating action is the clear, concise, and timely communications of potential problems to all customers, business partners, and other affected third parties, so they each can have adequate time to plan their own contingent actions. Each of these mitigating paths will demonstrate that the enterprise took the problem seriously and acted in the best interests of all concerned.

Finally, the book could be viewed as a partial blueprint for litigation. For an enterprise wishing to preview the course a year 2000 liability suit may take, the book has provided an outline of the actions required to demonstrate reasonableness. Consequently, the outline of topics can be used to formulate a defense or mount an attack. The choice is up to the reader.

APPENDIX A:
VENDOR LIABILITY AND THE YEAR 2000 CRISIS

Our last research bulletin examined the Y2000 problem from a macro level, examining what the Y2000 problem is, its impact on businesses, what you can do about it and some of the legal problems associated with it.

INPUT believes a more detailed look at the potential liability vendors face from this problem would be valuable since, as January 1, 2000 comes closer, an excess of litigation will spring up focusing on who is responsible for the problem and, more importantly, who is responsible for shouldering the cost of fixing it.

As part of our analysis, INPUT spoke with representatives from Arter & Hadden, a nationally recognized law firm specializing in information technology and business law. Legal views expressed here are theirs and are provided as an overview only. Specific legal questions regarding your company's precise liability should be discussed with a qualified attorney.

In the balance of this document, we consider some of the legal pitfalls you face in traversing these uncharted "liability" waters and how you can recognize and avoid them.

Reprinted by permission of INPUT, Systems Integration and Professional Services Program, Vol. vii, No. 3, April 1996.

This Research Bulletin is issued as part of INPUT's Systems Integration and Professional Services Program. If you have any questions or comments regarding this bulletin, please contact your local INPUT organization or Charles Billingsley at INPUT, 1921 Gallows Road, Suite 250, Vienna, VA 22182-3900, (703) 847-6870, FAX (703) 847-6872, E-mail: cbillingsley@input.com.

COPYRIGHT CONSIDERATIONS WHEN
PERFORMING MODIFICATION SERVICES

In addition to counseling and advising clients who face the Y2000 Problem, the IT markets for Y2000 services will consist primarily of programming services geared to upgrading and maintaining existing computer systems so as to make these systems Y2000 compliant.

If you, as an information services provider, choose to compete in this software upgrade and system maintenance market, always have your clients provide you with all information they have regarding the circumstances under which their systems were acquired, including development contracts, transfer documents, assignments and licenses. Review of this information is crucial because you must have a clear picture of the ownership/licensing status of the software you'll be working on before entering into an agreement to perform modifications.

Ownership status of computer software is vital in determining whether you or your client have the right to make modifications to a particular piece of software in order to achieve Y2000 compliance. Furthermore, you must determine whether your client has the right to hire someone other than the original software developer to perform the modifications.

Under U. S. copyright laws, computer software is considered a literary work. Therefore, the author of the software acquires a copyright for the software for either the life of the author plus fifty (50) years or, in the case of corporate authors, for seventy-five (75) years. (These periods of copyright ownership apply to computer software authorized after January 1, 1978.)

One of the exclusive rights afforded to authors under our copyright laws is the "right to prepare derivative works." A derivative work is a work based on one or more preexisting copyrighted works. Although the current case law is not clear, some believe that any modification which affects the functioning of a computer program will constitute the creation of a derivative work. The derivative work, of course, is the post-modification software program.

A corporation can be the author of a computer software program if the software was originally created as a "work for hire." A work for hire arises when the software is created by an employee of the corporation within the course and scope of his regular employment. In this instance, the company itself would be considered the author of the software.

If your Y2000 client has developed its own software "in-house," it is likely that the individuals who wrote the software were employees of your client at the time they wrote the software. In that case, as a "work for hire," the copyright in the software would belong to your client. As the owner of the copyright, your client has the ability and freedom to hire a third party to make whatever changes it chooses to the software.

If your client has licensed the software from the copyright owner, its ability to make (or hire you to make) modifications to the software will be controlled by the license agreement. It is likely that such a license will prohibit third-party modifications of the software. A thorough review of all licensing documents is advised prior to beginning *any* work.

In the event that your client is subject to a license which restricts its ability to modify the software, you or your client should first contact the original software developer to determine whether Y2000 compliant upgrades are available.

In the event that the original developer fails to offer Y2000 compliant upgrades, your client should seek to obtain that developer's permission to perform the necessary modifications. In the event such permission is not forthcoming, your client should consider some of the available legal remedies which are discussed below.

If the original developer does not provide upgrades and is unwilling to grant permission to your client to perform the modifications, seek advice from competent copyright counsel prior to embarking on a modification contract. This may help shield you from potentially enhanced liability for willful copyright infringement.

If the materials provided by your client show that your client neither developed the software at issue itself nor holds a license from the original developer, but actually owns the software outright, it is important to remember that even though your client may own the *software* it still does not own the *copyright* unless a valid copyright assignment has been made. If your client *owns* the software, but not the copyright, it may still have the right to perform limited Y2000 modifications under the copyright laws.

The Copyright Act grants "owners" of software programs the right to make or authorize the making of an adaptation of the computer program provided that such adaptation is created as an "essential step" in using the computer program in conjunction with a machine. In the event of Y2000 compliance, a very strong argument can be made that modifications relating to the Y2000 Problem are "an essential step" in using the program.

This is especially true if the program will become inoperative after December 31, 1999. However, further modification, which is not related to or necessary for the continued operation of the computer software, is not likely authorized under this statute and would be considered to be the creation of an unauthorized derivative work.

Other possible arguments a software owner might make to defend a claim of copyright infringement on the basis of modifications to ensure Y2000 compliance include fair use, the first sale doctrine, and a "private use" defense.

The Copyright Act provides that "fair use" can be made of copyrighted works. This means that an individual can engage in acts which are infringing under the statute, but that such acts are excused because of the circumstances of use.

The statute requires that four factors be considered in assessing whether a use is fair: (1) the purpose and character of the defendant's use of the copyrighted work; (2) the nature of the work; (3) the substantiality of the taking from the work; and (4) the effect of the defendant's use upon the market for the work.

In the Y2000 compliance context, if the original developer refuses to provide an upgrade or perform ongoing maintenance to cause software to become Y2000 compliant, a very strong argument can be made that modifications in order to achieve Y2000 compliance are "fair."

However, if the original developer provides upgrades or is providing maintenance services and you would be performing the modifications in competition with the original developer's business activities, it is much less likely that a court would find such use fair. Although the cases are somewhat unsettled on this topic, it would be advisable to get advice from counsel on a particular situation or to ask your client to indemnify you for possible copyright infringement claims.

The "first sale doctrine" provides that once an author of a work makes the first sale of a copy of that work, that author's rights are exhausted with regards to that particular copy. In the Y2000 compliance context, an argument can be made that a software developer has received the rewards of its work through payment for the original copy of the software purchased. This prevents a copyright owner from controlling the use to which the software is put after it has left his hands.

However, the application of the first sale doctrine in the instance of substantial modifications of the program is likely to be limited. Additionally, similar to the "essential step modification" discussed above, the first sale doctrine only applies to "owners" of copies of the software, not to mere licensees.

A third and final possible argument which could be made to defend a claim of copyright infringement is that of a "private use" defense. This is essentially an equitable defense that allows purchasers of software the right to use the software to satisfy the needs for which it was originally purchased; however, such a defense would exclude any commercial aspects to modifications which were made. It is likely that this type of argument would protect the client, but not the entity who is trying to market services related to Y2000 compliance.

Unfortunately, at this time, the copyright laws do not adequately address some of the unique problems associated with the protection of computer software. Different schemes have been proposed and discussed by commentators, but the law does not reflect many computer program-specific provisions.

Consider the issues outlined above carefully before entering into any contract to provide modification services. Protect yourself *and* your client by fully considering the intellectual property ramifications of the work that you do. If the owner of the copyright in the software determines that your Y2000 compliance activities are infringing, the time and expense of potential litigation can negate any benefits you may receive from entering the burgeoning Y2000 market for modification services.

OTHER LEGAL ASPECTS YOU SHOULD CONSIDER PRIOR TO ENTERING THE Y2000 MARKET FOR SERVICES

Most of the remaining legal issues which arise in connection with the Y2000 Problem in computer software concern general issues of contract and tort liability and are relevant in any transaction involving the sale of software.

Contractual Liability

Express Warranties

Contractual liability is based on breach of warranty. Warranties may be either expressed or implied. An express warranty is a statement presented as fact, a product description or a promise made concerning the software product. If these representations become part of the "basis of the bargain" between the parties to the contract, then these representations will be treated as an express warranty that the product will perform as represented.

In order to determine the scope of the warranties which accompany a software transaction, it is important to look at all transaction documents, product manuals or sales/marketing materials which may have accompanied the sale of the software.

In this event, a sales piece which states that, "This product will take you into the next century and beyond," may very well be treated as an express warranty that the product at issue is Y2000 compliant.

Whether or not these types of representations are considered to be part of a contract between the vendor and the ultimate software user depends on the terms of the contract between the parties. An effective disclaimer can usually be devised which will make clear that such statements are not assurances regarding the quality of the product and are not part of the sales contract.

In the instance of a shrink wrap license, it is unlikely that a disclaimer as to these types of warranties would be effective as courts are electing to prevent vendors from "giving with one hand and taking away with the other." However, if the contract consists of a sales document or license which was negotiated and executed by the parties as equal bargaining partners, courts are much more likely to allow disclaimers of warranties to stand.

It is important to continually review all advertisements and marketing pieces as well as to instruct your sales staff regarding the legal effect of the statements they make to your customers.

Implied Warranties

If your software transaction is governed by the Uniform Commercial Code (U.C.C.), which does not strictly apply to software programming services per se, but does apply to "goods" such as a computer system sold with software installed, two types of implied warranties may arise.

These warranties are the warranty of merchantability and the warranty of fitness for a particular purpose. These warranties are not triggered by representations on the part of the software vendor but arise by operation of law.

The warranty of merchantability provides that in every sale of goods there is a promise that the software is suited for the ordinary purposes for which such software would be used. That is, if a certain type of software would be expected to have a ten-year life span or would be used to calculate dates beyond the year 2000 in ordinary circumstances, failure to provide a Y2000 compliant product would constitute a breach of that warranty. An investigation must be made to determine the ordinary expectations of a user of this type of software prior to determining whether a breach has actually occurred.

The implied warranty of fitness for a particular purpose arises when the vendor has knowledge that the purchaser is buying the product in order to fulfill a particular need and that the purchaser is relying on the superior skill or knowledge of the vendor to procure the appropriate product.

This warranty is especially significant in instances in which the vendor is also serving as a software developer or as a consultant to the purchaser of the software. In the situation where a customer comes to a developer and asks for a particular type of system which would need to operate beyond the year 2000, failure of that developer to cause the system to by Y2000 compliant would constitute a breach of this warranty.

Both of these implied warranties may be disclaimed in a contract for the sale of the software if such disclaimer conforms to the requirements of the U.C.C. Otherwise, the disclaimer will be considered to be ineffective and liability can arise for breach.

Tort (Wrongful Act of Damage) Liability

Possible non-contract claims which might arise in a software transaction concerning a non-Y2000 compliant software product include: fraud and misrepresentation, fraud in the inducement, negligent misrepresentation, professional malpractice, negligent design, and strict liability.

Fraud and Misrepresentation

Tangentially connected to a claim for breach of express warranty, a claim for fraud and misrepresentation requires the purchaser to prove that the software vendor had intent to deceive and that the customer detrimentally relied on the deceptive representation. This type of claim is very difficult to prove and is many times precluded by a claim for breach of contract under express warranty if an intent to deceive cannot be shown. Additionally, as discussed above, a properly drafted contract disclaimer can greatly limit the potential liability stemming from express representations.

Liability for fraud arises just as it sounds: if you intentionally represent a system to be Y2000 compliant (when you know that it's not) in order to induce a purchaser to buy, liability for fraud can arise.

Fraud in the Inducement

A claim of fraud in the inducement can be made when a plaintiff believes that it was led to enter into a contract due to the fraudulent misrepresentations of the vendor. In instances where statements outside the contract are effectively disclaimed with regards to the performance of the software, a fraud in the inducement claim could still be made to seek recovery outside the contract altogether if the vendor intentionally misleads the customer regarding the contents of the contract. For example, a vendor could represent that the contract protects the customer (or provides a remedy against the vendor) from Y2000 problems when it really doesn't.

Negligent Misrepresentation

This cause of action is not available in all states, but in those states that do recognize it, a buyer is able to recover for a misrepresentation without being required to prove deceptive intent on the part of the vendor. Liability under this theory might arise if a vendor were to assure a customer that a particular system was Y2000 compliant without knowing whether this was true. If a plaintiff can show that the statement was, in fact, not true and the vendor should have reasonably known this, liability under this theory may arise.

However, liability under this theory may be limited because states which allow this cause of action usually require proof of a special relationship between the parties which gives rise to a duty on the part of the vendor to provide accurate and non-misleading information.

Professional Malpractice

Although this particular claim has not been fully litigated in the courts yet, it remains a viable claim in the instance of non-Y2000 compliant software, especially in the instance of custom designed software which is developed by specialized software firms.

Under this theory, "professionals" are held to a higher standard of care than ordinary vendors. A vendor who holds itself out as having special expertise or training in Y2000 issues may run into trouble if it fails to live up to its billing.

Negligent Design and Strict Liability

These two theories arise under a products liability theory of recovery. Accordingly, courts are usually reluctant to allow recovery under a negligent design or strict liability standard if only economic damage is alleged. However, in the instance where non-Y2000 compliance leads to the personal injury of an individual, design flaws inherent in the product could lead to a viable claim for negligent design or strict liability. The potential exposure for such claims in the event of an avionics software program or a medical equipment software program can be astronomical if Y2000 compliance is not immediately reviewed and remedied, if necessary.

HOW YOU CAN LIMIT YOUR POTENTIAL LIABILITY

Vendors

As discussed above, vendors can limit their potential contractual liability by disclaiming warranties. Express representations outside the contract can be limited by including appropriate integration and merger clauses. These clauses would state clearly that the terms of the contract control and that representations not contained in the contract are inoperative. However, such clauses do not bar the tort claims of fraud and misrepresentation as discussed above, so additional assurances must be sought from the customer to the effect that the customer did not rely on any representations outside of the contract when deciding to make the software purchase.

A liquidated damages provision can be included in all contracts provided that the estimate of damages stated in the contract is a reasonable estimate of damage incurred due to breach of contract. Recovery can also be limited to the repair or replacement of the software, in this case the upgrade or modification of the current software version to a Y2000 compliant version.

As long as these types of provisions are negotiated between the parties and are made explicit in the contract, courts are likely to let them stand. However, before entering into such an agreement you should have the agreement reviewed by competent legal counsel.

Placing similar limitations on product liability claims is much more difficult than the contract disclaimers for fraud and misrepresentation discussed above. However, these claims are also much more difficult for the plaintiff to prove and, hence, recovery is difficult. If you believe that you are facing exposure for potential tort liability, it is best to take immediate remedial measures in order to correct any perceived defects in the software due to non-Y2000 compliance.

For vendors, the road to the year 2000 is fraught with danger and potential liability. Attention to the niceties of copyright ownership and appropriate contracting and sales activities can make the transition much smoother. There is a tremendous business opportunity presented by the Y2000 problem. However, the potential for liability, if not addressed early, looms just as large.

Buyers

For software purchasers, you may be wondering now what you can do to protect your rights if you have made non-Y2000 compliant software purchases. There *are* effective ways in which customers can protect themselves from the above limitations of liability and recover damages which may result from defective software.

Many of the problems faced by computer software purchasers can be avoided by diligent negotiation and attention to contract drafting. Remember, you are the customer. In many instances a vendor will be willing to modify their standard contract (even if it is on a preprinted form) in order to get your business. If you are paying for a software system which should reasonably take you beyond the year 2000, you are entitled to assurance that you get what you pay for.

In the event that the software vendor attempts to limit all warranties express or implied in the contract, it is advisable to require the software vendor to provide *some* warranties stating that the software will meet some objectively determined performance criteria. Therefore, before entering into a software purchase contract, it is helpful to determine exactly what your expectations of the software's performance will be and make every attempt possible to include these terms in the contract.

Furthermore, if you *are* relying on any particular representations outside of the contract as the basis for your purchase, you should have those included by reference in the contract as well. For example, if you are relying on a copy of the user's manual to determine whether the software will perform in accordance with your needs, a reference in the contract incorporating the manual will serve as a warranty from the vendor that the software will perform as depicted in the manual.

Reference to external representations and documents can also serve as the basis for a claim for fraud, misrepresentation, or negligent design.

The purchaser of software should also make some provision for warranting future performance. This means that a purchaser of software should ensure it has a reasonable period in which to test and review the software in order to determine that such software conforms to the user's expectations and the representations provided in the contract. A test period should be provided to determine whether the software is Y2000 compliant. This is necessary because, even though the vendor may warrant that the system is Y2000 compliant and would therefore be liable under the contract if the system failed with the turn of the century, you can protect yourself from the disruption of your business if you are able to assess any deficiencies prior to that date.

If you would like further information about specific legal issues concerning the Y2000 problem or copyright regulations contact James L. Bikoff in the Washington, DC, offices of Arter & Hadden, (202) 775-7100.

APPENDIX B: YEAR 2000 DATE CONVERSION MANAGEMENT CONSIDERATIONS

Security issues and considerations must not be separated from the larger overall picture of the Year 2000 conversion problem. This problem poses one of the greatest threats that most businesses will ever encounter. It threatens the continued viability of any enterprise that has grown dependent on automation and it must be fixed, bypassed, or otherwise eliminated by the replacement systems. It cannot be ignored! To do so is to risk the business and allow for multitudes of legal and fiduciary complications.

A Year 2000 management methodology must emphasize testing. Multidisciplined teams will successfully accomplish the conversion. Special security considerations associated with a date conversion project must be incorporated.

ASSUMPTIONS AND CONSTRAINTS

The Year 2000 problem exists in all automation-dependent organizations. The degree of impact depends on the nature of the business and the importance that date data plays in the business process. In most organizations many of the following conditions must be considered in determining a solution to the Year 2000 date conversion problem:

1. Few organizations have performed a systematic risk assessment of the problem that takes into account the interrelated nature of all business

Reprinted by permission. Computer Security Handbook, 3rd Edition, 1997 Supplement, Arthur E. Hutt, Seymour Bosworth, and Douglas B. Hoyt, John Wiley and Sons, 1997.

processes both within the organization and among the business partners. Risks need to be assessed collectively, and solutions must serve the survival of the extended business family. Parochialism and an "everyone for himself" attitude can only guarantee damage to all.

2. Management has probably not budgeted adequately for this effort. Being in a general state of denial and with no sufficient risk assessment, the best that can be done is to quote the gross dollar estimates of consultants and industry study groups. The real significance of this lack of budget for a Year 2000 effort is that most other information technology (IT) budgets, especially for new systems, become vulnerable. Operations and maintenance budgets may be safe because the day-to-day show must go on, but plans for new productivity-enhancing systems may have to be cut back or eliminated until the date conversion is complete. The impact this will have on the individual business, while not desirable, is nothing compared to the negative impact it will have on the IT industry as a whole as procurements are cancelled and new software systems are stalled. There could be some very serious disruptions in the expected revenues of many IT contractors until the date conversion is completed and things get back to normal.

3. After more than a decade of information technology decentralization and proliferation, many organizations have no idea of the magnitude of the Year 2000 problem because no accurate inventory of computing assets exists. Only the organizations that have attempted to enforce some degree of standardization will have a baseline from which to project the problem scope, size, budget, and conversion strategy. Organizations that have allowed each business unit to pursue its own destiny for automation must now establish such baselines through the time-consuming activity of inventorying all computing assets and standardizing date data elements and date uses. Further, organizations have no control over the date conversion activities of their packaged software providers, of which there may be scores. Not all vendors have a long-term view that coincides with their customers' needs.

4. The seriousness of the Year 2000 date conversion problem is proving difficult to explain not so much from a technical perspective but from a political angle. After more than a decade of industry pronouncements that the mainframe is dead and the unprecedented spending to construct client/server and networked organizations, how does a CIO ask for the money to fix up antiquated legacy systems? After all, isn't business being conducted on these new expensive systems? Were not the mainframes supposed to go away? Why not just accelerate their exit? What do you

mean, the corporation is still highly dependent on these systems? We
didn't know that? Why didn't we know? What else don't we know? This
dialogue can only deteriorate from here and finger pointing may well
begin. No doubt about it, explaining how organizations got into this situation will be difficult and some unpleasant truths may surface.

5. Equally embarrassing will be the disclosure that much "legacy"
software is so poorly documented that just beginning to identify what
code has to be fixed will be a major undertaking.

6. The present IT staff is fully occupied either maintaining the current
undocumented legacy system or trying to deal with the complexity of developing new client/server and networked applications. Unless new technology efforts are stopped or slowed appreciably, with the staff being
diverted to the Year 2000 project (assuming the staff knows the mainframe
operating system, ALC, COBOL 68, VSAM, MVS, etc.), there is no one to
do the work. Outsourcing will have to fill the gap, and control of such a sensitive contracted task calls for unswerving executive commitment and
strong project organization and management. It is also likely that a Year
2000 conversion effort, essential as it is, will be subjected to unrelenting
pressures as scarce resources are directed away from system enhancement
programs to merely fixing those old antiquated "legacy" systems.

7. Many are wrongly assuming that the Year 2000 problem is primarily a problem of old software and "legacy" mainframe systems and does
not affect the PC and networked environments of the modern organization. On the contrary, all environments appear to be affected. Configurations are seldom standardized; as a result, each component of each
configuration needs to be tested separately, and then together.

8. Finally, time stops for no one. The world of IT and its customers
have become conditioned to schedule slippages. This time there can be no
slippage. Your Year 2000 date conversion project has a firm fixed date
which must be met.

SPECIAL SECURITY CONSIDERATIONS

The Year 2000 date problem poses obvious and subtle security concerns.
These concerns originate in the maturity with which the organization
currently manages computer security. A mature security program will
have performed computer system risk assessments in the past and will
already be aware of the adverse impact of a business processing interruption. Those companies that have never thought in terms of risk to their

automation support systems may not understand the impact of an interruption or the need for preventive and recovery actions. Security officials must warn corporate executives of the potential negative impact of an unresolved Year 2000 problem.

OBVIOUS YEAR 2000 SECURITY CONCERNS

By far, the most obvious and serious concern should be for continued viability of the business. If major core processes are interrupted, the loss in revenue and reputation may well prove catastrophic. Additionally, the expenses incurred to attempt a recovery after the fact will be overwhelming. Even small businesses, who may take a wait and see attitude, could find their computer dependence far greater than anticipated. These businesses would in turn suffer inordinate expense and inconvenience as they go about reconstructing their day-to-day operations and repairing client relations. Even those relying on software package suppliers to provide solutions need to analyze their situations carefully. These businesses should determine the actions that must be taken within the business to minimize any adverse consequences. Not all package vendors will respond in a responsible and timely manner to this challenge.

Beyond survival, the second most obvious security threat to the business will be the potential for legal entanglements as business obligations cannot be met. In an information-based economy these entanglements are extensive with most liability issues being largely unresolved. A system failure, or the transmission of inaccurate date-related data, resulting in a business loss to a customer will likely result in legal action. The same is true with information suppliers as their information products adversely impact their business partners and customers.

These two concerns must be candidly discussed at senior executive levels within the enterprise. Security officials and auditors must address these issues and lead the discussion to prevent the all-too-common practice of dealing with such issues solely at a technical level.

NOT SO OBVIOUS YEAR 2000 SECURITY CONCERNS

If the conversion is not accomplished in a timely manner, business failure and lawsuits will become more likely. As time passes, the ability to execute the conversion in an orderly fashion will diminish, shortcuts will be taken, and the likelihood of business failure and legal entanglements will only increase.

Even under the best of circumstances, security concerns during a conversion of this magnitude and in such a short time frame will include all the risks that accompany a relaxation of normal operational security and audit controls. Such risks could include the insertion of bogus data to files and confidentiality breaches of both corporate data and customer private information. There is also the heightened possibility of the insertion of viruses and unauthorized code that would go undetected until some future triggering date or event occurs. Shorten the time for conversion by delaying action and the relaxation of security and audit control will be even more complete and risks even greater. A relaxation of security and audit controls, a shortened conversion timeframe, and the use of outside Year 2000 service contractors may open a corporation to the entire spectrum of abuse and potential fraud.

SOLUTIONS

Assuming a reasonably mature level of security awareness and a functioning security program, the following actions will serve to prevent and mitigate the security concerns just cited.

1. Ensure that the Year 2000 inventory identifies sensitive applications programs and files. Treat them with greater security during the duration of the conversion.

2. Perform a business viability risk assessment during the start-up phase of the date conversion effort. Do not use an assessment previously accomplished to fulfill some security requirement. Such assessments will generally not adequately reflect the risk of a business interruption and certainly will not show the critical relationship between applications and outside information sources or destinations. A risk assessment to prioritize, by potential damage, the applications to be corrected is an essential step when time is short and only the most critical applications can be converted before January 1, 2000.

3. Prioritizing by potential damage will also allow applications to be partitioned for conversion work according to sensitivity. Sensitive partitions can be staffed by cleared personnel or specially trusted staff; while non-sensitive programs and files can be converted by noncleared personnel. Clearances are generally associated with defense or other sensitive government work, while bonding serves the same commercial function. Those who are cleared or bonded have passed background investigations and are deemed to be trustworthy.

4. The use of cleared or bonded persons should be considered if outside contractors or recruitments fill out a Year 2000 conversion team. If so, expect the per-person hourly rate to increase.

5. Be sure that data files are reviewed for overall accuracy before conversion begins. Many legacy systems have files that have grown over time and have not been periodically validated as to accuracy. If the file is inaccurate, a complete rebuild may be in order, or perhaps the system's necessity should be questioned. In any case, all date conversion data needs to be validated before returning the application to production.

6. Insist that testing be the main element of any Year 2000 conversion methodology. The process of finding and fixing date fields and coding logic must be validated through a rigorous test program that includes unit, module, systems integration, and business process testing. All tests at the business level need to be performed with security controls invoked in order to ensure both effectiveness of the conversion and efficiency from a performance and throughput perspective.

7. Before conversion efforts begin, ensure that all programs, documentation, and files are properly backed up so that reconstruction is possible should the unthinkable happen.

8. Mutual conversion agreements should be entered into with your information suppliers. Year 2000 product compliance should be enforced through contract language for all future acquisitions. Remember that it is imperative that security and audit officials participate in a Year 2000 conversion project and that a conversion model be employed by the organization only if it requires such participation.

THE TEST METHODOLOGY

The methodology to be discussed in the remainder of this paper is presented from a testing perspective and views a Year 2000 solution as requiring a multi-disciplined team effort with overall guidance and control coming from a highly placed program office. This discussion assumes that the constraints, conditions, and security concerns outlined in the previous section are recognized and that the complexity and urgency of the problem is honestly appreciated by the executives of the organizations. Conceptually, the process model is comprised of four phases (Figure B.1):

1. Identify where the date problem occurs, determine a "fix" strategy, and prepare conversion test environment.
2. Fix the problem in code and files and perform module and unit testing.
3. Test all fixes at the systems level.
4. Return to production and test.

These actions will be carried out through the efforts of a multi-disciplined Project 2000 Team. Some subordinate teams can tackle the problem on an application-by-application basis while other teams establish Year 2000 date conformance of the operating platforms upon which the applications reside.

Each Project 2000 Team should be considered dedicated to the effort with fully tested Year 2000 compliant systems as the final product. Actions of the team need to be coordinated around an integrated tool suite and use a standardized testing approach to deliver tested systems. Many different types of software tools can make up the suite. Tools can assist in documenting undocumented software code, finding date references, and determining the impact of the date references by tracing their use and flows across the system and sub-systems. Tools can be used to expand date fields, standardize date name references, and perform four-digit date compressions. Testing can be accelerated by tools at the module, unit, and systems test levels. Such tools can simulate Year 2000 date scenarios and perform regression and stress tests to determine operational impacts of date changes on other code and on system performance.

Full advantage from automated test tools will, however, be limited depending upon the extent to which such tools are already being used for

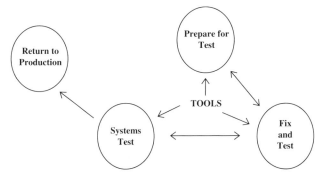

Figure B.1   Year 2000 Test Process Model.

ongoing routine software maintenance. If, for example, test cases and test routines, with their associated test data, have not previously been committed to an automated tool, valuable time and dollars will have to be spent doing so now. If, on the other hand, testing tools are being used in routine maintenance, automated libraries may only have to have minor modifications made to their test data for the date change tests to be carried out as routine maintenance.

Concurrency of action, while using the testing model, can be accomplished by employing an interactive fix/test/collaborate tactic. In this way, professional testers, working with programmers making the fix, can begin comprehensive module level and unit testing as soon as the code checkout is complete. This tactic will allow direct side-by-side communications between programmer and tester and should prove to be time-and-resource-efficient.

PARTICIPANTS

Preparation for Test

Building on the basic process model, Figure B.2 identifies the participants required to be full or part-time members of each Project 2000 team. As with most automation challenges, the quality of expertise and the amount of time allowed during the identification phase will determine the speed with which each subsequent phase can be completed. At a minimum, participants in the test preparation phase must include experts in the business application being examined, in-house or contract programmers knowledgeable about the software languages and DBMS

PARTICIPANTS

Prepare for Test	Fix and Test	Systems Test/Return to Production
Applications Experts	In-house Programmer	Application Expert
In-house Programmer	Contract Programmer	Test Engineer
Contract Programmer	Test Engineer	End-user Tester
Test Engineer		Auditor
Security Administrator		

Figure B.2   Year 2000 Process Model.

used by the application, the security administrator, testers experienced in comprehensive and performance testing, and personnel proficient with the chosen tool suite. It is essential, upon the completion of the identification of date conversion requirements, that the entire team analyze and determine a "fix" strategy consistent with the organization's overall Year 2000 date conversion policy. Time and resource estimates need to be refined based upon this strategy. All software and files surrounding the application need to be identified and their date conversion and test schedules need to be coordinated so that end-to-end business cycle testing can be planned and budgeted. Also important, if possible, is the establishment of the test environment as a mirror image of the existing software maintenance environment to include tools. If not already in place, configuration management must be established in order to track fixes and keep those fixes synchronized with the testing schedule.

Fix and Test

During this phase, the work falls primarily to programmers who will make the appropriate changes as determined by the strategy devised for the specific application. Test engineers will participate to ensure that changes are testable and to assist with support functions required to deliver properly documented logic changes. System test plans will be generated in cooperation with assigned programmers, and test cases and data developed if they do not already exist.

Systems Test

As stated previously, this particular Year 2000 methodology has been presented with heavy emphasis on the role of testing. Because of this emphasis, testers have been involved in the date conversion effort from the beginning, have supported the programmers in unit testing during the fix phase, and are now immediately capable of executing system tests following code release from the fix phase. Also participating during systems testing will be the applications expert who was involved during the preparation period, the end-user for operational and performance evaluations, and the auditor for ensuring that modified systems still satisfy prevailing certification requirements and industry standards.

Return to Production

Applications can be returned to production only after extensive business cycle testing. The period for this will depend upon the cycle itself, the complexity of the close-out transactions, and the reporting and database requirements of the application. Business cycle tests also require that inputs from outside the organization's direct control (i.e., a supplier) need to be date-compliant as well. Customers receiving outputs from your system's processing will also expect compliance. Careful advanced planning across business and industries will be required to coordinate this effort or appropriate conversion interfaces built.

INPUTS TO THE PROCESS MODEL

For the Project 2000 Team to successfully negotiate the four phases of the test process model in a timely manner, certain conditions must exist. At a minimum, the following inputs must be available to the project team:

- Application software documentation.
- User software documentation.
- System documentation to include input, output, process and data flow descriptions.
- Data element definitions.
- Database descriptions.
- Program language date field standards.

Additionally, all hardware platforms, including operating systems, and all networks need to be tested and certified as being Year 2000 compliant. Once again, it is important to remember that all date data information flows to any process be identified, including those originating and/or terminating outside the organization or company. Your business suppliers and any recipients of your information products must plan the date conversion together so that information flows are in harmony. Inter-organizational reviews should be initiated to insure that the Year 2000 effort of all business partners are synchronized.

To properly calculate the size of an organization's Year 2000 effort, estimating tools need accurate data concerning lines of code to be examined and an understanding of complexity usually rendered after running the code through a complexity analyzer. Needless to say, well-structured code will be easier to fix and test than unstructured code. This information is helpful not only to programmers responsible for effecting the fixes but also to the test engineers who are responsible for test planning and execution.

Without accurate and complete inputs during the preparation phase, the conversion task will be much more difficult and the outcome far more risky. In the interest of time, and before bringing a project team together, an organization may well want to examine the condition of the inputs and take action to bring them up to compliance with standards.

Figure B.3 describes the output to be delivered from each of the four phases of the Year 2000 test process model. Members of the Project 2000 team, using appropriate tools, will generate certain products from each phase. Products from the preparation phase center on locating as much date-related code and as many date fields, using tools as much as possible, and providing traceability for the outputs from date-manipulation algorithms. Test plans, procedures, and test data will be reviewed and updated if taken from the organization's inventory of existing test programs or developed new if they are not available. Test tool recommendations will be made or existing test tools will be readied for use.

Products from the Fix and Test phase will include expanded date fields in targeted programs, databases, and if necessary, modifications to the algorithms that maintain those date fields. Programming logic

PRODUCTS

Prepare for Test	Fix and Test	Systems Test/Return to Production
Location of Date Fields	Expanded Date Field	Validate Date Changes
How Date Field Is Used	Check Logic that Uses Date Field	Test Date Field Changes
Conditions that Change Date Field	Modify Logic and Test	Test Date Processing Logic
Established Test Environment	Document Changes Application	Regression Test
Test Plans, Cases, Data	Build Bridges and Document	Parallel Test Entire Application End-to-End

Figure B.3   Year 2000 Test Process Model.

that manipulates or otherwise uses date data fields may need to be modified and unit-tested. Finally, all changes must be brought under configuration management, tested, and documented.

Products from the Systems Test phase will be Year 2000 compliant code and databases turned back to production status. To do this, all date field changes in code or files must be tested through the use of the date-sensitive test scenarios that were developed in the preparation phase or are used in the course of code maintenance. Each application that experienced change will be regression-tested and finally a parallel (end-to-end) test of the application through an entire business cycle will be conducted. These final tests will draw heavily on end-user participation to insure realism and to minimize any adverse impact on the operational personnel of the organization. Auditor and security officer participation in these final operational tests is also required for any re-certifications that are necessary.

If time permits, an organization may desire to use independent evaluators to spot check applications coming out of the test phase. This would give an added degree of assurance and serve to keep the project teams motivated.

A YEAR 2000 MANAGEMENT PLAN OF ACTION

Use of the Year 2000 test process model with its four phases assumes that certain preliminary activities have occurred. Principal among these activities is the scoping analysis that must precede any determination of budgets and the setting of schedules. Initially, an inventory of affected software, systems, and data files must be performed. Estimates vary, but the Information Technology Association of America Year 2000 Committee projects the conversion cost per line of code to be near $1. Since this amount does not include comprehensive testing, $1.50 to $2.00 is probably more accurate, with some estimates rising to over $8 a line. Estimates are difficult to predict due to the many unknowns that cannot be answered until a conversion begins. For example:

- In what condition are software and systems documentation?
- How effective are existing configuration management, change control, and testing procedures?
- How will the use of automated tools figure into an overall strategy for the conversion? No tool is foolproof or in itself a complete conversion solution. Tool usage requires human interaction since it generates results which may or may not be accurate.

- Is testing a mature discipline within the organization or an activity generally carried out in an ad hoc fashion?
- Finally, has the organization done its internal planning with regard to the conversion, or will programmer and testing personnel be sitting around while basic strategy decisions are being made?

The following activities should be undertaken and managed for a Year 2000 conversion to succeed:

Preparatory Actions

1. Establish a project management office with appropriate authority and prepare a Year 2000 Conversion Plan.
2. Conduct inventory.
   —Applications
   —Hardware platforms
   —Files and databases
   —Networks and workstations
3. Perform business impact analysis.
   —Intra-business impacts
   —Inter-business dependencies and impacts
4. Classify risks and prioritize applications to be converted.
   —"Real-time" operational
   —"Core" business processing
   —Legal requirements
5. Establish resource budget for conversion.
   —Pilot project
   —Full conversion and testing
6. Establish conversion environment.
   —Hardware resources
   —Software tools
   —Programmers (i.e., contract)
   —Test engineers (i.e., contract)
7. Institute conversion management processes and procedures.
   —Conversion work flow defined
   —Find and fix procedures, including corrective action strategy determination and dispute resolution
   —Validation, verification, and test procedures

—Configuration management and change control process
—Data administration
—Documentation procedures

Implementation

1. Update Year 2000 conversion plan.
2. Establish conversion teams.
3. Identify date locations in code and files.
4. Establish configuration management and change control.
5. Expand or compress fields.
6. Correct software logic.
7. Build bridges and document.
8. Perform validation testing.
9. Perform system regression testing.
10. Perform integration testing.

Return Systems to Production

1. Phase-in corrected systems.
2. Bring up bridge systems and test.
3. Perform end-to-end business cycle acceptance testing.
4. Perform stress testing.
5. Maintain configuration management and change control.
6. Finalize documentation.
7. Return software to maintenance.

CONSIDERATIONS AND ADDITIONAL BENEFITS

There is nothing new in the approach outlined in this paper for those experienced with software conversions and systems maintenance. What is new is the extent to which a Year 2000 conversion affects all aspects of information technology and the enterprise it supports. Few businesses are fully aware of the extent to which they have become dependent on automation and modern communications. The Year 2000 conversion will force such companies to identify these dependencies in order to accomplish the conversion and keep their business running. Beyond survival, however, other benefits should accrue that have long-term impacts on the future use of information technologies and may also assist in justifying the expense and inconvenience of the Year 2000 conversion.

First, the process of inventorying the information system assets of the enterprise and their prioritization for conversion should result in a valuation determination that may never have been made before. Such determinations can create a type of "general ledger" perspective concerning automated information assets that is needed to manage them just as other corporate assets are managed. Such an analysis will allow more effective capital investment decisions to be made regarding future uses of technology; in the past such decisions may often have been made without a clear understanding of the benefits the technology would bring even though investments were very large.

Second, the identification of information flows and process relationships required during a Year 2000 conversion can uncover areas for potential business process re-engineering improvements. This side effect of the conversion analysis could contribute significantly to planned modernization efforts.

Third, an opportunity exists to improve relations with information providers to the enterprise and with those to whom the enterprise supplies information. The requirement to identify date data flows beyond the enterprise and to coordinate date conversions with other organizations sets the stage for overall information and product quality improvements between all parties following ISO-9000 standards and other quality management guidelines.

Fourth, having just been forced to deal with software products resulting from the immature and undisciplined developments of the past, the organization will better understand the importance of pursuing future software developments from an engineering perspective.

CONCLUSIONS

As the world's businesses begin to understand the urgency of the Year 2000 conversion, IT suppliers will offer a great many solutions. It is doubtful that any easy solutions will surface and, even if they did, assurances must still be given to management, boards of directors, stockholders, and government regulatory bodies that systems are indeed ready for the Year 2000. Such assurances can only come through rigorous testing performed by professional testers using a well-defined methodology.

SUGGESTED REFERENCES

Beizer, B. *The Frozen Keyboard: Living with Bad Software*. Blue Ridge, PA: Tab Books, 1988.

Birrell, N. D. and Ould, M. A. *A Practical Handbook for Software Development*. Cambridge University Press, 1985.

Braithwaite, T. *The Power of IT-Maximizing Your Technology Investments*. Milwaukee, WI: ASQC Quality Press, 1966.

Braithwaite, T. *Information Excellence Through TQM*. Milwaukee, WI: ASQC Quality Press, 1994.

Charette, R. N. *Application Strategies for Risk Analysis*. New York: McGraw-Hill, 1990.

Charette, R. N. *Software Engineering Risk Analysis and Management*. New York: McGraw-Hill, 1989.

Eason, K. *Information Technology and Organizational Change*. London: Taylor and Francis, 1992.

Jones, K. *Year 2000 Software Crisis-Solutions for IBM Legacy Systems*. Boston: International Thomson Computer Press, 1997.

Keough, J. *Solving the Year 2000 Problem*. London: Academic Press Limited, 1997.

Mandell, S. *Computer, Data Processing and the Law*. St. Paul, MN: West Publishing Company, 1984.

Marks, D. M. *Testing Very Big Systems*. New York: McGraw-Hill, 1992.

Meilir, P. *Practical Project Management-Restoring Quality to DP Projects and Systems*. New York: Dorset House Publishing, 1985.

Murray, J. T. and Murray, M. J. *The Year 2000 Computing Crisis—A Millenium Data Conversion Plan*. New York: McGraw-Hill, 1996.

Neumann, P. G. *Computer Related Risks*. New York: ACM Press (a division of the Association for Computer Machinery, Inc.), 1995.

Optner, S. L. *Systems Analysis for Business Management.* Englewood Cliffs, NJ: Prentice Hall, 1968.

Royer, T. C. *Software Testing Management: Life on the Critical Path.* Englewood Cliffs, NJ: PTR Prentice-Hall, Inc., 1993.

Ulrich, W. and Hayes, I. S. *The Year 2000 Software Crisis—Challenge of the Century.* Englewood Cliffs, N. J.: Yourdan Press Computing Series, 1997.

Weinberg, G. M. *Quality Software Management, Volume 1: Systems Thinking.* New York: Dorset House Publishing, 1992.

Whitten, J. L., Bentley, L. D., and Barlow, V. M. *Systems Analysis and Design Methods, 2nd ed.* Homewood, IL: Irwin Press, 1989.

Yourdan, E. *Structured Walkthroughs.* Englewood Cliffs, N. J.: Yourdan Press, 1979.

INDEX